GENERAL EDITOR
Professor Solomon H. Snyder, M.D.
*Distinguished Service Professor of
Neuroscience, Pharmacology, and Psychiatry at
The Johns Hopkins University School of Medicine*

•

ASSOCIATE EDITOR
Professor Barry L. Jacobs, Ph.D.
*Program in Neuroscience, Department of Psychology,
Princeton University*

•

SENIOR EDITORIAL CONSULTANT
Joann Rodgers
*Deputy Director, Office of Public Affairs at
The Johns Hopkins Medical Institutions*

THE ENCYCLOPEDIA OF PSYCHOACTIVE DRUGS

SERIES 1

SERIES 2

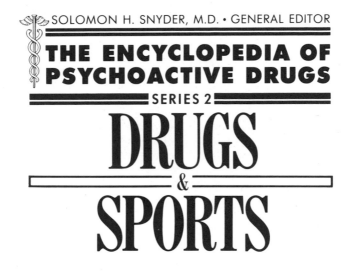

SOLOMON H. SNYDER, M.D. • GENERAL EDITOR

THE ENCYCLOPEDIA OF PSYCHOACTIVE DRUGS

SERIES 2

DRUGS
&
SPORTS

JEFF MEER

CHELSEA HOUSE PUBLISHERS
NEW YORK • PHILADELPHIA

A note regarding the pictures in this book: Unless specifically stated in captions or text, none of the athletes in this book are involved in the use of illicit drugs or the misuse of legitimate drugs. No picture in this volume is intended to suggest — nor should it be taken as suggesting — substance abuse on the part of those pictured.

EDITOR-IN-CHIEF: Nancy Toff
EXECUTIVE EDITOR: Remmel T. Nunn
MANAGING EDITOR: Karyn Gullen Browne
COPY CHIEF: Perry Scott King
ART DIRECTOR: Giannella Garrett
PICTURE EDITOR: Elizabeth Terhune

STAFF FOR DRUGS AND SPORTS:

SENIOR EDITOR: Jane Larkin Crain
ASSOCIATE EDITOR: Paula Edelson
ASSISTANT EDITOR: Michele A. Merens
DESIGNER: Victoria Tomaselli
COPY EDITORS: Sean Dolan, Gillian Bucky
PICTURE RESEARCH: Juliette Dickstein
PRODUCTION COORDINATOR: Alma Rodriguez

COVER: Liane Fried

Library of Congress Cataloging-in-Publication Data
Meer, Jeff.
   Drugs & sports.
   (Encyclopedia of psychoactive drugs. Series 2)
   Bibliography: p.
   Includes index.
   1. Doping in sports—Juvenile literature. I. Title.
II. Title: Drugs and sports. III. Series.
RC1230.M44   1987   613'.71   87-753

ISBN 1-55546-226-X
     0-7910-0794-4 (pbk.)

CONTENTS

Children are influenced by a variety of external forces in their lives. Since sports heroes have traditionally served as inspiring role models for younger fans, the use of drugs among athletes can have a profoundly negative influence on youngsters.

In the Mainstream of American Life

One of the legacies of the social upheaval of the 1960s is that psychoactive drugs have become part of the mainstream of American life. Schools, homes, and communities cannot be "drug proofed." There is a demand for drugs — and the supply is plentiful. Social norms have changed and drugs are not only available—they are everywhere.

But where efforts to curtail the supply of drugs and outlaw their use have had tragically limited effects on demand, it may be that education has begun to stem the rising tide of drug abuse among young people and adults alike.

Over the past 25 years, as drugs have become an increasingly routine facet of contemporary life, a great many teenagers have adopted the notion that drug taking was somehow a right or a privilege or a necessity. They have done so, however, without understanding the consequences of drug use during the crucial years of adolescence.

The teenage years are few in the total life cycle, but critical in the maturation process. During these years adolescents face the difficult tasks of discovering their identity, clarifying their sexual roles, asserting their independence, learning to cope with authority, and searching for goals that will give their lives meaning.

Drugs rob adolescents of precious time, stamina, and health. They interrupt critical learning processes, sometimes forever. Teenagers who use drugs are likely to withdraw increasingly into themselves, to "cop out" at just the time when they most need to reach out and experience the world.

Fans in the stadium are as much a part of a game's excitement as its players. Too often, however, enjoyment of a sporting event is dampened by those spectators who drink to excess and become violent.

Fortunately, as a recent Gallup poll shows, young people are beginning to realize this, too. They themselves label drugs their most important problem. In the last few years, moreover, the climate of tolerance and ignorance surrounding drugs has been changing.

Adolescents as well as adults are becoming aware of mounting evidence that every race, ethnic group, and class is vulnerable to drug dependency.

Recent publicity about the cost and failure of drug rehabilitation efforts; dangerous drug use among pilots, air traffic controllers, star athletes, and Hollywood celebrities; and drug-related accidents, suicides, and violent crime have focused the public's attention on the need to wage an all-out war on drug abuse before it seriously undermines the fabric of society itself.

The anti-drug message is getting stronger and there is evidence that the message is beginning to get through to adults and teenagers alike.

The Encyclopedia of Psychoactive Drugs hopes to play a part in the national campaign now underway to educate young people about drugs. Series 1 provides clear and comprehensive discussions of common psychoactive substances, outlines their psychological and physiological effects on the mind and body, explains how they "hook" the user, and separates fact from myth in the complex issue of drug abuse.

Whereas Series 1 focuses on specific drugs, such as nicotine or cocaine, Series 2 confronts a broad range of both social and physiological phenomena. Each volume addresses the ramifications of drug use and abuse on some aspect of human experience: social, familial, cultural, historical, and physical. Separate volumes explore questions about the effects of drugs on brain chemistry and unborn children; the use and abuse of painkillers; the relationship between drugs and sexual behavior, sports, and the arts; drugs and disease; the role of drugs in history; and the sophisticated drugs now being developed in the laboratory that will profoundly change the future.

Each book in the series is fully illustrated and is tailored to the needs and interests of young readers. The more adolescents know about drugs and their role in society, the less likely they are to misuse them.

Joann Rodgers
Senior Editorial Consultant

British track star Sebastian Coe (right) takes the lead in this 1984 Olympic qualifying race. Drug use by athletes has indeed become a problem of worldwide proportions. Nonetheless, most athletes, such as Coe, continue to rely on inner strength and talent to succeed.

The Gift of Wizardry
Use and Abuse

JACK H. MENDELSON, M.D.
NANCY K. MELLO, Ph.D.
Alcohol and Drug Abuse Research Center
Harvard Medical School—McLean Hospital

Dorothy to the Wizard:

"I think you are a very bad man," said Dorothy.
"Oh no, my dear; I'm really a very good man; but I'm a very bad Wizard."
—from THE WIZARD OF OZ

Man is endowed with the gift of wizardry, a talent for discovery and invention. The discovery and invention of substances that change the way we feel and behave are among man's special accomplishments, and, like so many other products of our wizardry, these substances have the capacity to harm as well as to help. Psychoactive drugs can cause profound changes in the chemistry of the brain and other vital organs, and although their legitimate use can relieve pain and cure disease, their abuse leads in a tragic number of cases to destruction.

Consider alcohol — available to all and yet regarded with intense ambivalence from biblical times to the present day. The use of alcoholic beverages dates back to our earliest ancestors. Alcohol use and misuse became associated with the worship of gods and demons. One of the most powerful Greek gods was Dionysus, lord of fruitfulness and god of wine. The Romans adopted Dionysus but changed his name to Bacchus. Festivals and holidays associated with Bacchus celebrated the harvest and the origins of life. Time has blurred the images of the Bacchanalian festival, but the theme of drunkenness as a major part of celebration has survived the pagan gods and remains a familiar part of modern society. The term "Bacchanalian Festival" conveys a more appealing image than "drunken orgy" or "pot party," but whatever the label, drinking alcohol is a form of drug use that results in addiction for millions.

The fact that many millions of other people can use alcohol in moderation does not mitigate the toll this drug takes on society as a whole. According to reliable estimates, one out of every ten Americans develops a serious alcohol-related problem sometime in his or her lifetime. In addition, automobile accidents caused by drunken drivers claim the lives of tens of thousands every year. Many of the victims are gifted young people, just starting out in adult life. Hospital emergency rooms abound with patients seeking help for alcohol-related injuries.

Who is to blame? Can we blame the many manufacturers who produce such an amazing variety of alcoholic beverages? Should we blame the educators who fail to explain the perils of intoxication, or so exaggerate the dangers of drinking that no one could possibly believe them? Are friends to blame — those peers who urge others to "drink more and faster," or the macho types who stress the importance of being able to "hold your liquor"? Casting blame, however, is hardly constructive, and pointing the finger is a fruitless way to deal with the problem. Alcoholism and drug abuse have few culprits but many victims. Accountability begins with each of us, every time we choose to use or misuse an intoxicating substance.

It is ironic that some of man's earliest medicines, derived from natural plant products, are used today to poison and to intoxicate. Relief from pain and suffering is one of society's many continuing goals. Over 3,000 years ago, the Therapeutic Papyrus of Thebes, one of our earliest written records, gave instructions for the use of opium in the treatment of pain. Opium, in the form of its major derivative, morphine, and similar compounds, such as heroin, have also been used by many to induce changes in mood and feeling. Another example of man's misuse of a natural substance is the coca leaf, which for centuries was used by the Indians of Peru to reduce fatigue and hunger. Its modern derivative, cocaine, has important medical use as a local anesthetic. Unfortunately, its increasing abuse in the 1980s clearly has reached epidemic proportions.

The purpose of this series is to explore in depth the psychological and behavioral effects that psychoactive drugs have on the individual, and also, to investigate the ways in which drug use influences the legal, economic, cultural, and even moral aspects of societies. The information presented here (and in other books in this series) is based on many clinical and laboratory studies and other observations by people from diverse walks of life.

Over the centuries, novelists, poets, and dramatists have provided us with many insights into the sometimes seductive but ultimately problematic aspects of alcohol and drug use. Physicians, lawyers, biologists, psychologists, and social scientists have contributed to a better understanding of the causes and consequences of using these substances. The authors in this series have attempted to gather and condense all the latest information about drug use and abuse. They have also described the sometimes wide gaps in our knowledge and have suggested some new ways to answer many difficult questions.

One such question, for example, is how do alcohol and drug problems get started? And what is the best way to treat them when they do? Not too many years ago, alcoholics and drug abusers were regarded as evil, immoral, or both. It is now recognized that these persons suffer from very complicated diseases involving deep psychological and social problems. To understand how the disease begins and progresses, it is necessary to understand the nature of the substance, the behavior of addicts, and the characteristics of the society or culture in which they live.

Although many of the social environments we live in are very similar, some of the most subtle differences can strongly influence our thinking and behavior. Where we live, go to school and work, whom we discuss things with — all influence our opinions about drug use and misuse. Yet we also share certain commonly accepted beliefs that outweigh any differences in our attitudes. The authors in this series have tried to identify and discuss the central, most crucial issues concerning drug use and misuse.

Despite the increasing sophistication of the chemical substances we create in the laboratory, we have a long way to go in our efforts to make these powerful drugs work for us rather than against us.

The volumes in this series address a wide range of timely questions. What influence has drug use had on the arts? Why do so many of today's celebrities and star athletes use drugs, and what is being done to solve this problem? What is the relationship between drugs and crime? What is the physiological basis for the power drugs can hold over us? These are but a few of the issues explored in this far-ranging series.

Educating people about the dangers of drugs can go a long way towards minimizing the desperate consequences of substance abuse for individuals and society as a whole. Luckily, human beings have the resources to solve even the most serious problems that beset them, once they make the commitment to do so. As one keen and sensitive observer, Dr. Lewis Thomas, has said,

> There is nothing at all absurd about the human condition. We matter. It seems to me a good guess, hazarded by a good many people who have thought about it, that we may be engaged in the formation of something like a mind for the life of this planet. If this is so, we are still at the most primitive stage, still fumbling with language and thinking, but infinitely capacitated for the future. Looked at this way, it is remarkable that we've come as far as we have in so short a period, really no time at all as geologists measure time. We are the newest, youngest, and the brightest thing around.

DRUGS
&
SPORTS

The tragic, cocaine-related death of University of Maryland basketball star Len Bias in 1986 shocked the nation and vividly dramatized the fact that athletes were not immune to the deadly effects of drugs.

AUTHOR'S PREFACE

To many people throughout the United States, the death of Len Bias came as a devastating shock. What really happened to the University of Maryland basketball standout in the early morning of Thursday, June 19, 1986, may never be known. But one thing remains clear: Bias, perhaps the best basketball player ever to put on a uniform at Maryland, died of an overdose of cocaine.

Some other facts are known. Bias was 22 years old at the time of his death. He was 6 feet 10 inches tall, weighed 220 pounds, and was by all accounts in remarkably good physical shape. He came from a stable home and had many friends.

Furthermore, on June 17, 1986, the Boston Celtics had made Bias their first-round draft pick — the second pick overall in the prestigious National Basketball Association (NBA) draft. The following day, representatives of a major sports-shoe manufacturing company had met with him to discuss his promoting their products in Massachusetts, a lucrative deal that would have augmented the already astronomical salary the Celtics were offering him. Bias was on the verge of attaining the dream pursued by thousands of other young athletes across this country. Len Bias was going to be a professional athletic superstar.

Hercules was a hero of ancient Greek mythology and paragon of strength and athletic skill. Hoping to enhance their "merely human" abilities, athletes of ancient Greece ate hallucinogenic mushrooms before many competitions, including the original Olympic Games.

What happened? On one level, the answer is as straightforward as it is heartbreaking. After meeting with the shoe company and signing with the Celtics, Bias returned to the campus in College Park, Maryland. That night he and his friends decided to celebrate his good fortune. During their party Bias apparently smoked (or "freebased") a quantity of relatively pure cocaine. The strain on his heart caused by the drug was monumental, and Bias succumbed to a massive heart attack sometime in the next several hours.

It would be easy to say that Bias was an isolated example of an athlete who for one reason or another turned to drugs. But he is far from alone. Just 10 days after the Bias tragedy, Don Rogers, a 6-foot-1-inch, 206-pound free safety with the Cleveland Browns of the National Football League (NFL), died of a cocaine overdose. Only 23 years old, he was to have been married the following day.

Although tragic, these deaths have served a purpose — they have forced all of us, athletes and spectators alike, to consider the connection between drugs and sports. As psychiatrist Robert Millman puts it, "Throughout history almost every society has used psychoactive substances for medical, religious or recreational purposes." Perhaps suprisingly, given their investment in physical prowess and well-being, athletes have always been as prone to drug abuse as any other members of society. As any given drug finds its way into the mainstream of a particular culture, that drug will be abused in the athletic community as well as elsewhere. In fact, there is even evidence to suggest that, for a variety of reasons, drug use may be proportionately even *higher* among athletes than among the population in general.

As early as the 3rd century B.C.E. (before the common era; equivalent to B.C.), Greek athletes ate psychotropic (mind-affecting) mushrooms before competing in the original Olympic Games, hoping to better their abilities. Later, gladiators in the Roman Circus Maximus (an arena in ancient Rome where chariot races and gladiator fights were held) used certain stimulants to continue to fight, even after being injured.

During the late 19th century, when opium abuse was epidemic in both Europe and the United States, marathon runners took this drug — a common narcotic containing morphine — in combination with other substances to help them ignore the pain that can accompany long-distance running. Runners also tried using sulfate of strychnine, a popular but potentially deadly stimulant in doses as low as one-sixtieth of a grain, to boost performance.

Runners were not the only ones to try popular, albeit dangerous, drugs. In 1896 Welsh cyclist Arthur Linton, winner of the famed 1886 race from Bordeaux to Paris, reportedly died of typhoid fever. Tom Donohoe and Neil Johnson report in their book *Foul Play: Drug Abuse in Sports*, however, that it is likely that Linton succumbed to the disease, in part, because he was weakened by repeated doses of strychnine administered by his trainer during races. This trainer, "Choppy" Warburton, was eventually officially banned from the sport for life.

Later, other drugs became popular in society, and most of these, as we shall see in later chapters, also found their way into sports. Drug use among athletes continues in contemporary society, perhaps at rates higher than at any other time in history.

Why Do Athletes Take Drugs?

To be sure, many athletes take drugs for a variety of over-lapping reasons. Basically, their motives can be divided into three categories: "recreation," performance enhancement, and pain relief. (We are referring here to drug *abuse*, of course, and not legitimate medical use.) This volume will investigate the relationship between drugs and sports according to these three broad categories.

When an athlete (or anyone else) takes a drug just to "get high," or "have fun," we call this *recreational* use. Alcohol, tobacco, caffeine, marijuana, and cocaine all qualify as recreational drugs in this context because in the 1980s their primary use by athletes has nothing to do with performing better in athletics. In fact, even when it does not result in serious health problems or death, use of any of these substances hampers overall athletic performance.

Most recreational drugs are relatively easy to obtain. Despite the best efforts of law-enforcement officials, there is evidence that illicit drugs are as openly available on many city street corners as the legal drugs alcohol and tobacco are in retail stores. In theory, at least, marijuana and cocaine are illegal substances, and alcohol and tobacco are not supposed to be available to minors, but that rarely seems a barrier to those who want them. One sports physician, Forest Tennant, Jr., M.D., who is an NFL drug adviser and also the drug consultant to baseball's Los Angeles Dodgers, estimates that up to half of all athletes who are 25 years old have been exposed to drugs — the same percentage as among their nonathlete peers.

Even if drugs of this type are easy to get, some of them — particularly cocaine — are relatively expensive and for this reason often appeal to those moving in the glittery and glamorous fast lane of professional entertainment and sports. Their expense poses less of a problem for highly paid professional athletes, many of whom, while they are still in their early 20s, make vast sums of money. For less successful athletes, getting the kind of money necessary to buy cocaine can lead to criminal activities that, quite apart from the harmful effects of the drug, are themselves dangerous.

Drugs that enhance performance are called *ergogenics*. The desire for speed, more stamina, and greater strength is always present among athletes. As the Medical Commission of the International Olympic Committee (IOC) noted in its *Manual on Doping*, "The merciless rigor of modern competitive sports, especially at the international levels, the glory of victory and the growing social and economic rewards of sporting success increasingly force athletes to improve their performance by any means available."

Athletes of every era seek to improve upon the records of those who came before them. For example, one researcher calculated that in the average distance event in track and field, the runners get faster by two and one-half feet per minute every year. Various different studies have shown that the maximum work output of the average athlete is 20% greater today than it was 40 years ago. As *New York Times* writer Frank Litsky has noted, "Ultimates are guaranteed to survive—until they are broken."

In 1985 former New York Yankee Joe Pepitone was arrested on charges of cocaine possession. Highly paid athletes are sometimes tempted by a "fast track" life that can include experimenting with drugs.

It seems little wonder that the fastest proliferation of new drugs is in areas that are thought to allow athletes to improve their performances. These drugs include amphetamines and other stimulants as well as steroids and related compounds (some of which represent the very leading edge in biogenetic engineering) used to promote extraordinary muscle and body growth. These drugs are also relatively easy for athletes to get, yet none has been shown conclusively to help athletes perform. Even more important, they have been implicated in a wide range of adverse physical problems.

Painkillers and the minor tranquilizers that artificially relax the body are classified as *therapeutics*. Athletes sometimes abuse these drugs so that they can continue performing at or near their peak even after injury or return to competition before they are physically and/or mentally ready to do so. As with all drugs that offer artificially quick solutions to problems that require longer-term therapy, the therapeutic drugs can only mask symptoms temporarily and can sometimes contribute to devastating, permanent damage.

Spectators and coaches expect top athletes to be able to "play with pain." When NBA center Bill Walton was forced out of a game by an excruciatingly painful foot injury, he was

Although some athletes look to drugs to help them cope with pressure and to improve their performances, Shirley Strong, winner of an Olympic silver medal in the hurdles, shows that the most inspiring feats are accomplished by sheer talent and drive.

Lightweight boxer Carlos "Teo" Cruz lost his title when a championship fight was stopped because of this severe cut on his eye. Some athletes use drugs to dull pain so that they can continue to compete, even though it may be dangerous to do so.

jeered by many insensitive and ignorant "fans." Some people, it is true, are able to function with pain levels that would incapacitate others, but when the level of discomfort endured is confused with "worth," ability, or courage, some athletes are bound to dull the pain of their injury with therapeutics and return to competition prematurely. This situation can turn them into well-respected cripples. (For more details on Bill Walton's injury see Chapter 4.)

The drugs discussed in this volume are found on street corners, in medicine cabinets, and in liquor stores. They are found in physicians' offices and in trainers' lockers. They are found in lists of banned substances maintained by international and national sports agencies regulating both amateur and professional sports.

Sometimes they are found, on autopsy, in the body of an athlete.

This book is for athletes and nonathletes alike. It is for anyone who loves sports and is concerned that athletic competition is being corrupted by drug abuse.

Champagne and cigars have become regular features of exuberant victory celebrations. Here, Rollie Fingers, ace relief pitcher for the Milwaukee Brewers, savors the win that clinched a share of the American League East title for his team in 1981.

CHAPTER 1

ALCOHOL, NICOTINE, AND CAFFEINE

Even though the destructive properties of alcohol, nicotine, and caffeine are well known, their abuse continues to be widespread in contemporary society. They are used — consciously or unconsciously — to manage stress, to overcome exhaustion, to enhance leisure time. Athletes, who in their work routinely endure brutalizing competition and the challenge to perform, are as vulnerable as anyone else to the seductive yet dangerous allure of these legal substances. Also, because they are in such good physical condition, many athletes may find it easy to believe that they have a special immunity to the damage these substances can do to flabbier, more sedentary men and women. Of course, alcohol, nicotine, and caffeine can undermine even the most godlike athletic heroes, but a special vanity may blind them to this simple truth.

The Most Commonly Abused Drug

Although many people do not think of alcohol as a psychoactive drug, beer, wine, and hard liquor are really the most commonly abused drugs in the United States. Alcohol is different from some of the other substances discussed in this book in two important respects: it is legal and socially ac-

Long-distance runner Gabriel Andersen-Scheiss fought off heat and exhaustion to finish the 1984 Olympic marathon. Runners should never drink alcoholic beverages before a race because this produces substances that cause excessive heat in the body.

ceptable to use. But this does not mean that alcohol is not dangerous. By some estimates, there are 10 million "problem drinkers" in this country, and 3.3 million of them are between the ages of 14 and 17. It is difficult to define exactly what a problem drinker is, but one way to find out is to ask people. In the fall of 1985 the Gallup organization asked a national sample of teenagers if their own use of alcohol had ever been a source of trouble in their lives. One in eight replied that it had caused problems.

As discussed earlier, athletes do not differ from most people in terms of the drugs they use. For example, a survey of the football team at Baker University in Baldwin City, Kansas, found that 90% of the players drank regularly. Such statistics are not limited to athletes at small liberal arts colleges. A 1982 survey of 1,000 male football players, basketball players, swimmers, and track athletes competing in the Big Ten athletic conference, conducted by officials of the National Collegiate Athletic Association (NCAA), found that 36% drank during the season and more than half drank during the off-season.

The active ingredient in alcohol is ethyl alcohol, or ethanol, also known as "grain alcohol," which is made from the fermented juices of grains, fruits, and berries. There are other chemical compounds known as alcohols (wood alcohol, rubbing alcohol, and butanol), but none is commonly drunk the way grain alcohol is. Contrary to what many people believe, alcohol is chemically a depressant rather than a stimulant. In other words, it tends to slow, rather than stimulate, brain cells.

The reason people who drink seem to gain energy, often becoming hyperactive and overly aggressive, is that alcohol depresses centers of social control in the brain. Temporarily, alcohol can make some people more vivacious and outgoing. It can also turn ordinarily mild-mannered people into aggressive loudmouths and lead to a deadly recklessness among those who drive after they have had "one too many."

Bars are popular gathering places for fans who like to watch sports events on television. In turn, games on television are periodically interrupted by advertisements for wine and beer, further encouraging spectators to associate alcoholic beverages with competition.

Under the influence of alcohol, communication among brain cells is lessened. Even in the first stage of intoxication, drinkers feel slightly less coordinated. After a few more drinks, self-control is more seriously weakened. In some cases of extreme intoxication, drinkers can lose consciousness. Prolonged drinking can cause the part of the brain that controls breathing to stop functioning. This can lead to coma and death.

Alcohol and Athletics

Alcohol is normally absorbed into the body through the lining of the stomach and small intestine. It acts upon many of the body's systems, but especially relevant to the athlete are the effects on the central nervous system. Numerous studies have documented that hand-eye coordination, reflexes, and sense of balance suffer after only a drink or two. Perhaps most important, a few drinks can cause a person to lose the ability to recognize and react to sensory perceptions such as sight, sound, or touch. This means that drinking before participating puts athletes at a serious disadvantage in fast-paced sports such as basketball, football, tennis, auto racing, and hockey, all of which require coordination and timing.

There is some evidence that drinking can interfere with the body's ability to rid itself of excess heat. Alcohol can generate a lot of excess heat, for example, in the body of an athlete who is participating in an endurance sport such as long-distance running. This situation can be unhealthy and sometimes dangerous. Because of the nature of their temperature-regulating system, female athletes are especially at risk.

Why might a competitor drink before a game or a race? In addition to the changes in the central nervous system, drinking alcohol creates, however temporarily, a feeling of well-being or relaxation in most people. An athlete might be tempted to "take the edge off" by having a drink, especially before a championship match or a big game. (See also Chapter 4 on benzodiazepines and beta-blockers.) Although some choose to drink before participating, all of the available evidence shows that alcohol does not enhance athletic performance and may make it worse. Researchers at the University of Tennessee tested the effects of moderate drinking on the athletic ability of six people who usually did not drink and six who did. Not surprisingly, they found that drinking did not help endurance or make it any easier to pedal a bicycle for either group. They also found that drinking did not substantially reduce the blood pressures or heart rates of the cyclists, an indication that alcohol did not affect the athlete's level of tension.

Other researchers have tested muscular and aerobic abilities of certain athletes after drinking. The American College of Sports Medicine (ACSM) summarizes the research this way: "Alcohol appears to have little or no beneficial effect on the metabolic and physiological responses to exercise. Furthermore, in studies reporting significant effects, the change appeared to be detrimental to performance."

It does not look as though using alcohol immediately before an athletic event is a good idea. Temporary gains in relaxation and confidence do not compensate for ultimate losses in coordination and reflexes.

These exhausted decathlon participants exemplify the tremendous physical endurance some sports require. Drinking alcohol does not improve endurance; moreover, it impairs coordination and reflexes.

What about athletes who drink the night before participating, just to enjoy themselves? No athlete wants to play his or her most important game with a hangover and take the risk that the nausea, headache, and general malaise associated with "the morning after" might contribute to poor performance. In fact, drinking a great deal can make sleeping difficult, leaving the drinker weak and tired the following day.

Aside from these common problems, however, no one really knows much about the long-term effects of moderate drinking on athletic ability. Some of the only information we have on these effects comes from research on animals. Researchers at the University of Texas at Austin taught rats to swim and then fed them daily doses of alcohol. After several weeks, the researchers measured the rats' muscular ability; interestingly, the muscles the rats used for swimming seemed to have been unaffected by the alcohol, but other muscles had withered and atrophied (decreased in size). Whether the same physical deterioration occurs in human athletes is as yet unknown. In any case, the ACSM recommends that adult athletes drink no more than three bottles of beer, four glasses of wine, or three ounces of whiskey in any one day.

"Absolute Animals"

There is every indication that the relationship between alcohol and sports extends widely beyond the athletes themselves. Beer companies purchase commercial time on television broadcasts; vendors hawk beer at baseball games; Mexican soccer players and fans both drink pulque (a drink made of the fermented juices of the agave fruit) during a match; British dart players and their ale-drinking audiences are legendary. The relationship between athletics and alcohol use by participants and spectators is clearly evident and knows no cultural or national boundaries.

In recent years it has become clear that alcohol not only causes physical problems directly but also is involved in the ugly behavior of sports spectators. In May 1985, 39 fans were killed in Belgium after a violent brawl erupted between followers of a British soccer team and those of its Italian opponent. The incident, which resulted in a yearlong ban against British teams playing regular-season games in Europe, was

Thirty-nine people died in riots started by fans of rival teams at this 1985 soccer match in Brussels, Belgium. Many attribute the violence to heavy alcohol consumption in the stands.

not caused by alcohol but was probably worsened by the fact that many of the fans had been drinking.

Similarly, on August 7, 1986, a ferry captain was forced to lock up some of his passengers after a drunken brawl among 150 rival soccer fans en route from England to a game in the Netherlands resulted in three stabbings. He turned the boat around and headed back to Harwich, England, where police made 14 arrests. Following the game 200 more supporters had to be shipped back to England under police escort after they drunkenly broke windows and vandalized stores in downtown Amsterdam. Peter Bruinvels, a Conservative member of the Dutch Parliament, called the delinquents "absolute animals."

The Brutality of Alcoholism

The consequences of chronic heavy drinking are, sadly, well known. Alcoholism is one of this country's major health problems, and it affects athletes and nonathletes with equal brutality. As with any other drug, heavy use of alcohol can lead to dependence (physiological or psychological need for a substance to the extent that emotional or physical disturbances occur when the substance is withdrawn) and mental as well as physical breakdown. Increased irritability and delirium tremens, or "DTs" (hallucinations, disorientation, and tremors), are common symptoms. Alcoholics are also prone to liver damage, muscle degeneration, and a host of neurological and psychiatric disorders.

Some sociologists have suggested that alcohol can become as much of an obsession to some athletes as sports themselves, but research at the University of Georgia indicates that, health and fitness aside, there are important psychological differences between athletes and alcoholics. In the University of Georgia study, a group of 159 runners (who in their obsessive commitment to their sport might be said to be "addicted" to it) was found to be more emotionally stable, independent, and in control than a group of 141 alcoholics.

Kenny Anderson, former quarterback of the Cincinnati Bengals, was among several celebrities who appeared in "Coffee Achievers" commercials, part of a multimillion-dollar advertising campaign launched by the coffee industry in 1983. Although caffeine, which is the active ingredient in coffee, can improve endurance, it does not make an athlete stronger or faster.

Members of the latter group, by the same token, were shown to be dependent on others, more often emotionally unstable, and impulsive.

"Sick and Tired"

Throughout the modern era of sports, star athletes in games as diverse as baseball and darts have been well-known drinkers. Babe Ruth, Grover Cleveland Alexander, and Hack Wilson are just a few baseball giants who were known as heavy drinkers.

Anyone not convinced that getting drunk is a bad idea for an athlete ought to listen to former Cleveland Indian star pitcher Sam McDowell. The youngest pitcher ever to strike out 300 batters in a season (in 1965), "Sudden Sam" Mc-Dowell was also a problem drinker. "I was the biggest, most hopeless and most violent drunk in baseball during my 15 years in the majors," he told the *Washington Post*. By 1975 he had been traded a third time, to the Pittsburgh Pirates, and was known as a "problem drinker." Although he had promised to keep his drinking under control, he "celebrated [a big victory] all night," he says. "Next day I'm in the bullpen and coach Don Leppert sees me still crazy drunk and takes me into the clubhouse." Thirty seconds later McDowell was fired. "I didn't want to join another team," he says, "because I was afraid they would try to stop my drinking."

McDowell got help and was able to kick the alcohol habit. He now spends his time helping other athletes stop drinking. "I knew I had this habit but I didn't know it was an illness. I didn't know I had been lying to myself all those years and that I had one of the worst diseases known to mankind. All I knew was that I was sick and tired of being sick and tired."

"The Most Addictive Drug"

Nicotine is the active agent in cigarette, cigar, and pipe smoke as well as in smokeless tobacco. First used by Europeans in the 16th century, tobacco and a burgeoning interest in cultivating it were two of the motivating forces behind the settlement of the Americas. By 1977 the tobacco industry in the United States was worth more than $16 billion, and the surgeon general estimated that cigarette companies spent more than $779 million on promotional advertising for their industry.

About a third of all adults say that they smoke. Although this is a decrease from the peak year of 1966, when 43% said they smoked, it is still high enough to rank nicotine as a highly abused recreational drug. Most people learn to smoke when they are in their teens, usually as a result of peer pressure, the influence of cigarette advertisements, or because they imitate their parents or other role models such as actors, singers, and other celebrities. More than 1.7 million teenage girls and 1.6 million teenage boys were smokers in 1979, according to government statistics, and more than 13% of American high school seniors smoke half a pack a day.

There are, of course, athletes who smoke and chew tobacco. In Virginia a survey of high school athletes indicated that about a fifth smoke regularly. If the survey data is reliable, almost as many chew tobacco, making the total use of tobacco among high school athletes about the same as it is among the general population. More experienced athletes also smoke at comparable rates, although there seems to be a great variability according to sport and level of ability. A French study, for instance, reported that 40–50% of professional rugby and soccer players smoke. Interestingly, the same study reported that none of the professional cyclists studied were smokers, and neither were any members of the 1980 French Olympic team.

What Does Nicotine Do?

The effects of nicotine are puzzling. On the one hand, people who smoke say they do so to relax, and, indeed, one of the effects of nicotine is to stimulate the Renshaw cells in the spinal cord, which in turn relax many of the body's muscles. On the other hand, another effect of nicotine is to stimulate (or quicken) many bodily functions. Within ten seconds of being inhaled (and a few more seconds after being chewed) nicotine enters the brain. In a complex series of events, it acts quickly upon the adrenal gland, causing it to release adrenaline and noradrenaline, hormones that stimulate many other bodily systems. This action raises the heart rate and blood pressure, increases arousal and general excitement, and raises the respiration rate so that the smoker breathes more quickly. The drug affects the central nervous system directly by interfering with the electrical impulses in the brain's cortex (or covering layer), and it triggers the release of vasopressin and beta-endorphins. Vasopressin (also known as antidiuretic hormone — ADH) slows down the elimination of water from the body; beta-endorphins can block the body's ability to sense pain.

It is possible to become physiologically dependent on nicotine. People who have smoked for years have difficulty quitting for many reasons, but one is that they greatly miss the drug's action on their nervous system. If smokers become accustomed to the stimulation and euphoria produced by a cigarette, they may suffer a "rebound" effect when they try to quit — they are likely to be lethargic and irritable until their bodies adjust to functioning without the drug. (Many smokers also dread giving up their habit because they fear gaining weight.)

Smoking also has important effects on the vascular or circulatory system. It immediately reduces the amount of oxygen that goes to the heart, since some of the oxygen normally carried there by the blood is replaced by carbon monoxide, another gas found in cigarette smoke. At the same time, smoking increases the heart's demand for oxygen and also causes many of the blood-transport system's main avenues to constrict, making the flow of blood slower.

Pure nicotine is actually quite poisonous. Even smokers may be surprised to know that a drop or two, about 50 milligrams (mg), can kill a person in minutes. If one were foolish enough to eat a full-strength cigarette, the 15–20 mg of nicotine it contains could be lethal or at least might produce serious physical and mental reactions.

Nicotine and Athletics

Some people feel that the stimulating effects of nicotine help them concentrate during an athletic event. Other athletes enjoy smoking before competing because of the relaxing effects of the drug. British researcher S. Miles assessed the fitness of 337 men, some of whom were smokers. "There are even top class athletes who find that a quiet cigarette before the ordeal has a steadying effect on the nerves," he says.

But these competitors may not be aware of the array of

negative effects that smoking has on performance. One West German study, for example, found that smoking three cigarettes in 30 minutes, even among those who have never smoked before, causes a 14% decline in overall athletic performance. Another showed that athletes who smoked a single cigarette had pulse rates that were up to one-third faster and blood pressures up to 20% higher, even before they began competing. A Polish study found that if athletes smoked only 5 cigarettes a day for 40 days, their level of physical fitness could plummet by as much as 40%.

Beyond these specific statistics, there is evidence that smokers simply do not perform as well, on average, as do nonsmokers. For example, 137 new recruits in the West German army were asked to run as far as possible in 12 minutes. The smokers covered an average of 2,323 meters (2,540 yards), while the nonsmokers ran more than a football field farther — an average of 2,459 meters (2,690 yards). Smoking's detrimental effects are not limited to the extremely active. The Metropolitan Life Insurance Company did a thorough examination of 764 men who worked for the company from 1969 through 1975. After jogging, rowing, bicycling, and doing sit-ups for 90 seconds each, the men recorded their pulse rates at one-minute intervals. The pulses of the nonsmokers returned to normal much faster than did those of the smokers. The results of this study and others with similar findings are usually interpreted to mean that the cardiovascular systems of nonsmokers have greater capacities than those of smokers. Nonsmokers, therefore, should be better able to deal with the stresses of everyday life, not to mention athletic competition, than smokers.

Deadly Effects

Young people who smoke succumb to minor illnesses more frequently and recover from them more slowly than those who do not. Of course, the real dangers of cigarette smoking for both athletes and nonathletes come much later. Nicotine use has been implicated in a host of cardiopulmonary (heart and lungs) conditions, including high blood pressure.

It is impossible, however, to divorce the effects of nicotine from the general effects of smoking. Other long-term dangers from smoking may have more to do with tar and other materials in tobacco than with nicotine itself, but the

Baseball players Harvey Kuenn (left) and Rocky Bridges demonstrate a popular pastime among athletes: chewing tobacco. Studies show that smokeless tobacco can cause cancer of the tongue, mouth, and gums.

problems they cause are just as important. Smokers are at great risk of developing bronchitis and cancers of many kinds (especially lung cancer). In fact, it is commonly stated that heavy smokers live an average of 8.3 fewer years than non-smokers.

The litany of long-term effects is grim indeed. Smokers have higher cholesterol levels and higher blood pressure than do nonsmokers. Their endocrine (system of ductless glands that secrete hormones directly into the blooodstream) and digestive systems do not function as well, and there is some evidence that their muscle strength may be lower. Of course, smoking also complicates pregnancy and can do permanent damage to an unborn child.

In the 1980s many high school students — aware of the risks of smoking — began "chewing" tobacco, placing a bit between the cheek and gum, instead of smoking it. Although tobacco is not as detrimental to the lungs when used this way, chewing small packages, sometimes called "bandits," still

A 1975 Michigan court order banned smoking in sports stadiums. As this photograph of fans at a Detroit Lions game indicates, at least one person wholeheartedly approved of the decision.

places extremely high levels of nicotine in the body, with concurrent risks. In addition to the circulatory problems they share with smokers, those who chew tobacco face a very real danger of cancer of the mouth, gums, or tongue. Four dentists from Texas examined 14 varsity baseball and football players in a small college town, all of whom used chewing tobacco or snuff. Nine players, all between 18 and 22 years old, were diagnosed as already having leukoplakia — a cancerlike disease of the lining of the mouth.

The late Senator Robert Kennedy once eloquently summed up the effects smoking has on athletes or anyone else. "Every year cigarettes kill more Americans than were killed in World War I, the Korean War and Vietnam combined; nearly as many as died in battle in World War II," he said. "Each year cigarettes kill five times more Americans than do traffic accidents. Lung cancer alone kills as many as die on the road. The cigarette industry is peddling a deadly weapon. It is dealing in people's lives for financial gain."

Caffeine

Imagine two groups: four coworkers in an office sharing a coffee break and four teenagers sharing a bottle of tequila. At first glance, the groups appear to have little in common, but actually both are doing similar things—using drugs.

As discussed earlier, alcohol is a rather potent drug. Similarly, caffeine, the active component in coffee, tea, cocoa, many soft drinks, some pain relievers, and chocolate, is a stimulant drug that is capable of large-scale effects on the body.

Caffeine in the form of coffee and tea has been used for hundreds of years by people all over the world. The average cup of coffee contains 90 mg of caffeine. (Decaffeinated brands contain up to 5 mg per cup.) Some soft drinks contain up to 50 mg of caffeine in a 12-ounce (oz.) serving, while others contain less (1.5 mg). Most major brands of brewed tea contain less than 90 mg per 5-oz. cup. Some pain relievers, such as Excedrin and Anacin, also contain caffeine (65 mg and 32 mg per tablet, respectively) and an 8-oz. carton of chocolate milk contains up to 7 mg. Finally, caffeine is available in tablets such as No Doz (100 mg) and Vivarin (200 mg), made specifically to increase alertness.

The United States government estimates that our country consumes about 1 billion kilograms (2.2 billion pounds) of coffee every year. Most people eat or drink about the equivalent of several hundred milligrams of caffeine per day, although about three in a hundred people consume 600 mg every day. A fatal dose of caffeine is about 10 grams or 10,000 mg. Caffeine, a stimulant, is absorbed very rapidly. Within about a half hour of being consumed, it reaches its strongest concentration in the bloodstream. Depending on the individual, its half-life (the period of time it takes the body to eliminate half of what has been consumed) ranges from about 3 to 10 hours.

The bloodstream carries caffeine to the central nervous system. Once there, the drug promotes the release of adrenaline, which increases the heart rate and sometimes elevates blood pressure, especially during periods of stress. Users can become hyperalert, or — if they consume large enough doses — agitated, anxious, and unable to sleep. Caffeine also reaches the digestive system, where it stimulates the lining of the stomach to release gastric acid and encourages the kidneys to produce urine.

Caffeine and Athletics

In 1978 researcher David Costill reported that if athletes drank two to three cups of coffee an hour or two before competition, they could perform up to 20% longer before becoming fatigued. He showed, for example, that cyclists did 7% more work over two hours and cross-country skiers completed a 23-kilometer (14.3-mile) race up to 3% faster.

Recent research has indicated that this may be due to the way caffeine affects the body's means of producing energy. The body stores energy in two principal forms: glycogen and fats. Normally, when a muscle is activated, it first metabolizes (or burns) glycogen, the most readily available energy form, by allowing it to react chemically with oxygen from the bloodstream, releasing energy. The process is known as aerobic respiration. The body is able to metabolize glycogen even if there is not enough oxygen present. "Oxygen debt" occurs when the body uses glycogen without oxygen (anaerobic respiration) for energy and produces a byproduct called lactic acid. Some researchers believe that it is the accumulation of lactic acid in the muscles that causes athletes to become fatigued. The body recovers from fatigue by chemically combining lactic acid with oxygen when it becomes available, for example, when an athlete hyperventilates or breathes hard, after a race.

Caffeine's action alters this process. It is believed that the drug allows the body to release fats into the blood, in a form known as free fatty acids, and burn them instead of burning glycogen. In this way the body avoids having to use glycogen. The buildup of lactic acid in the muscles and the fatigue it brings is therefore postponed.

Other research on caffeine has established that the drug does seem to help in endurance sports, but it may be less useful to other athletes. For example, cyclists may be able to pedal longer, but they cannot pedal any faster after consuming caffeine. Of course, since caffeine may increase athletic performance, the International and United States Olympic committees ban competitors from consuming abnormally high amounts before competing. We will examine this issue at greater length in the chapter on drug testing.

Caffeinism

At moderate levels caffeine increases alertness and talkativeness and decreases fatigue. Consuming 350 mg a day or more, however, can lead to a form of physical dependence sometimes referred to as "caffeinism." Regular use of 600 mg a day or more has been associated by some researchers with chronic insomnia, breathlessness, anxiety, depression, and upset stomach. In fact, very high levels for prolonged periods can mimic severe psychological disturbances.

Regular coffee drinkers who decide to stop using caffeine often complain of painful headaches. Recently a research group led by Solomon Snyder at the Johns Hopkins University School of Medicine discovered that this effect is due, at least in part, to caffeine's interaction with a body chemical called adenosine. One of adenosine's many functions in the body is to act as a depressant, inducing nerve cells (including those in the brain) to stop firing, or transmitting signals. According to Snyder, caffeine seems to block this effect, allowing the nerve cells to continue stimulating other cells and thus raising the level of activity in the body. If a person regularly consumes too much caffeine, however, the body responds by becoming more receptive to adenosine. If the person suddenly stops consuming caffeine, the adenosine already present in the body causes the extrasensitive blood vessels in the head to expand rapidly, causing a headache.

The potential dangers of caffeine have been widely discussed. There are those who believe that even moderate levels of caffeine can cause heart problems and forms of cancer. Although there is no concrete proof for these allegations, it is obvious that, as with alcohol, caffeine should be used in moderation, if at all. Especially for pregnant women, people with heart conditions, or those with ulcers, drinking no more than three cups of coffee a day, or consuming the equivalent amount of caffeine in other substances, is a good general rule. Caffeine use presents an additional risk for athletes, since consumption of too much of the drug can result in the same disqualification they might receive for using two more serious recreational drugs—marijuana and cocaine.

All-star outfielder Dave Parker was one of nearly two dozen athletes embroiled in a scandal concerning the use of cocaine among major league baseball players in the late 1970s.

CHAPTER 2

MARIJUANA AND COCAINE

Although alcohol and nicotine are addictive, potentially dangerous psychoactive substances, they are more socially accepted than are marijuana and cocaine. These last two are not only potent and harmful, but illegal.

Why should this be so? After all, marijuana was smoked as a medicine as early as 2737 B.C.E. in China, and cocaine was chewed in the form of coca leaves by the Incas in Peru as early as 600 C.E. (common era; equivalent to A.D.) Perhaps society's special disdain for these drugs stems from the fact that before the 1960s, use of either in the United States was confined mostly to the underprivileged, those in the entertainment world, and criminals — in other words, those outside the mainstream of conventional society. When marijuana became widely popular among young people during the late 1960s, the drug came to stand for a generation known as the "counterculture" — made up of people who scorned convention and rejected traditional values. Cocaine, now a widely abused drug, was relatively unknown in this country between the 1920s and the late 1970s.

Although there is some evidence that use of both these drugs declined somewhat in the mid-1980s, both still qualify as massively abused drugs and enormous health hazards. Unfortunately, both are still widely used by athletes.

Marijuana

The marijuana plant is grown all over the world but grows best in hot, dry climates such as those in central Asia. Normally, the upper leaves and flowering tops of the plant are picked and cured before being smoked. Sometimes hashish, a more purified form, is also smoked.

More than half of all high school seniors in 1983 had tried marijuana at least once, making it by far the most frequently used illicit substance in the United States. About a quarter of those students said they had gotten high in the last month, and about 5% claimed they got high every day. These numbers are high but are somewhat lower than they were in 1978, when about 10% said they used the drug daily.

The main psychoactive compound in marijuana is delta-9-tetrahydrocannabinol (also known as THC), a strong hallucinogen that passes easily from the lungs into the blood and the brain. THC stays in the body a fairly long time and can accumulate in the bodies of those who smoke frequently since it attaches readily to fat cells and other body lipids (fats or fatlike substances characterized by their insolubility in water and solubility in fat solvents such as alcohol). Reports from laboratories all over the country show that the THC content of marijuana has increased eightfold in the last few years and some samples (called sinsemilla) now exceed 10%. Hash oil (oil extracted from hashish) may contain between 15% and 30% THC.

The Short-Term Effects

Most people smoke marijuana to experience its euphoric properties, including relaxation, intensification of perception, and visual fantasies. Some athletes say that they use marijuana following a sporting event because it allows them to feel relaxed and at peace.

Marijuana, however, also has some immediate negative effects. Occasionally, even experienced marijuana smokers report feeling panicky or anxious after smoking a particularly strong joint or getting high in unfamiliar surroundings. Most of marijuana's psychoactive properties usually last no more than a few hours.

Almost immediately after marijuana is smoked, a user's heart rate increases dramatically, up to 50% higher than normal. Also, the tiny blood vessels in the eyes dilate (enlarge), and the whites of the eyes take on a reddish hue. Many people who get high report that they become ravenously hungry or extremely drowsy within about 15 minutes of smoking marijuana. Smoking can also cause the throat and mouth to become dry.

Marijuana and Athletics

Curiously, despite the significant effects of THC on the body, most people who smoke marijuana feel that they can function just as well under the influence of the drug as they can "straight." Study after study, however, has documented that people under the influence of marijuana perform poorly on virtually every sort of mental and physical task.

For example, the increase in heart rate after smoking decreases the body's maximum tolerance for exercise and makes the smoker more vulnerable to fatigue. In addition, although THC dilates the bronchial tubes leading to the lungs, the smoke that is inhaled causes the same tubes to constrict. This makes breathing, particularly the labored breathing of an athlete in action, more difficult.

Marijuana also has significant effects on the central and peripheral nervous systems. After smoking, people have poorer memory, slower reflexes, and a distorted sense of time. They are also likely to have poorer vision, since THC interferes with depth perception, peripheral vision, and the ability to track an object across a visual field.

These effects can last substantially longer than the euphoric state does. Tests of driving ability, for instance, have shown that the complex motor skills necessary for driving remain impaired for at least 10 hours, at least 4 hours longer than the sense of relaxation. One study by Canadian researchers found that marijuana is at least as dangerous for drivers as drinking. In another recent study, Stanford University Medical Center psychiatrist Jerome Yesavage and psychologist Von Otto Leirer asked 10 experienced amateur pilots to land an airplane (using a simulator) before and after smoking a moderately strong dose of marijuana, and virtually all the pilots had trouble landing an hour after smoking. Yesavage invited the pilots back the next day, and many still had significant problems even though 24 hours had passed since they smoked. In fact, Yesavage notes that one pilot landed

Cleveland Indians pitcher Len Barker was arrested in the summer of 1982 for allegedly smoking marijuana on a Chicago street corner. Barker denied the charges and was released on bail in time to play a game the next evening.

completely off the runway. "It certainly would make you think twice about doing a complex task such as landing a plane," he says.

Nonetheless, some athletes do smoke marijuana. In March 1986, 15% of 335 top college football players eligible for the NFL draft later in the year tested positive for THC in a training camp. Baseball and basketball players in the United States have also been known to get high. In May 1986 Great Britain's Test and County Cricket Board banned 30-year-old Ian Botham, one of the world's best cricket players, because he admitted in an interview that he occasionally smoked marijuana.

The Biggest Drug Problem

As with cigarettes, marijuana smoking has been linked to far-reaching problems. Regular smokers are likely to develop bronchitis and other respiratory problems, since the irritants and carcinogens (substances causing cancer) in marijuana smoke are present in amounts that are even greater than those found in tobacco products.

Careful study of marijuana use is comparatively new. One potential consequence of daily smoking that has emerged recently is perhaps more troublesome than any other. There is evidence that those who smoke often, especially if they begin as teenagers, may be prone to a "chronic cannabis syndrome." According to psychiatrist Sidney Cohen, the syndrome consists of loss of energy, reduced levels of drive and ambition, apathy, depression, agitation, and withdrawal from previous interests. Obviously, the implications for athletes are disastrous. Although most experts believe that the syndrome can be reversed after several months of abstinence, the athlete may have permanently lost his will to compete.

People who smoke regularly gradually develop a tolerance to the effects of the drug. In a study that followed regular users for five years, smokers said that the positive effects — such as the feelings of relaxation, peacefulness, and self-confidence — gradually decreased. Interestingly, even though they felt that the pleasurable sensations had lessened, those in the study said they smoked just as much as they had five years earlier. There is a mild withdrawal effect when regular smokers quit using marijuana, but this appears to be a psychological reaction rather than a physical reaction. Marijuana "addicts" are those who try to keep an effective level in the blood 24 hours a day. Since it takes the body about five days to eliminate THC from the system, those who get high every day have it in their body at all times.

Exactly how bad is marijuana for athletes? Physican Forest Tennant, Jr., believes marijuana is the biggest drug problem in sports. According to Tennant, the consultant to the Los Angeles Dodgers and the NFL on drug problems whom we mentioned earlier, "It [marijuana] ends more players' futures than do all other drugs and alcohol combined."

Cocaine

The list of professional and amateur athletes who have become involved with cocaine reads like an index of broken dreams. In early 1986 Micheal Ray Richardson of the New Jersey Nets was banned from the NBA because of drug use.

In April 1986 Quintin Dailey, a guard for the Chicago Bulls, voluntarily asked for time off to correct his drug problems. Dailey had admitted himself to a rehabilitation center in October 1985 and was released a month later, only to reenter the center in February. In January 1987 Lewis Lloyd and Mitchell Wiggins of the Houston Rockets were also banned from the NBA after having tested positive for cocaine. The banned players can apply for reinstatement after two years. (The specifics of the NBA's assault on drug use among its players will be discussed in detail in Chapter 5.)

Football has not been immune to the cocaine problem. Don Reese, a former member of the Miami Dolphins and San Diego Chargers, discussed the NFL/cocaine connection in a 1982 article in *Sports Illustrated* magazine. Reese, who had served a one-year prison sentence, received $10,000 for the article. "What you see on the tube on Sunday afternoon is a

There is a substantial history of cocaine abuse among professional basketball players. Joe Bryant, a forward with the Philadelphia 76ers, was arrested in 1976 for cocaine possession. He is seen here entering court with his daughter.

lie," he wrote. "When players are messed up, the game is messed up. The outcome of games is dishonest when playing ability is impaired." (Reese had to return to jail as a result of writing the article, in which he admitted associating with drug dealers — a violation of his parole.) Reese is certainly not the only cocaine user ever to wear a football uniform. Carl Eller, a former defensive lineman for the Minnesota Vikings, estimates that 40% of NFL players regularly use the drug. In the same pre-NFL draft camp in which some players tested positive for marijuana use, 3 of the 335 potential professionals also tested positive for cocaine use. When former Miami Dolphin standout Mercury Morris was freed from prison in June 1986, he had already served 3 years of a 20-year sentence imposed on him after he pleaded no contest to charges that he was involved in a cocaine conspiracy. In July 1986 the New Orleans Saints were forced to withdraw their contract offer to tailback Barry Word, a third-round draft choice from the University of Virginia, after he admitted selling small amounts of cocaine. "His career is over here, if he ever had a career here," said Jim Finks, the Saints' general manager, who also expressed his regrets.

In a 1986 article in *Time* magazine NFL Commissioner Pete Rozelle explained why so many of the players in his league have used cocaine: "Professional athletes are an ideal target for drug use," he said. "They fall within the susceptible age group, 20 to 35. They receive inordinate salaries. They have free time due to the short length of the professional sports seasons, as much as six months."

Cocaine and Baseball

The sport that has become most closely identified with cocaine, at least in the news media, is baseball. In January 1986 Peter Ueberroth, commissioner of Major League Baseball (MLB), summoned 21 players to his office. These athletes had been implicated in a drawn-out trial in 1985 in Pittsburgh concerning cocaine sale and use by the Pirates and other teams during the late 1970s. Fans across the country were stunned to learn that Ueberroth had imposed penalties on the players, including mandatory drug testing for the rest of their careers, the choice of up to one-year suspension or the donation of up to a tenth of a year's salary to a drug prevention

New York Mets all-star first baseman Keith Hernandez dodges a pitch. One of the outstanding players in the league, Hernandez was nevertheless in danger of losing the respect of fans and colleagues alike when he was implicated in the major league cocaine scandal in 1985.

program, and community service. Two of baseball's biggest stars, former most valuable players Keith Hernandez, a member of the New York Mets, and Dave Parker, a Cincinnati Red, were among those involved.

All 21 players eventually complied with Ueberroth's sanctions, even though many thought the penalties too harsh. Lee Lacy, a Baltimore outfielder, paid a fine of $34,250 rather than face a 60-day suspension. "I'm glad it's behind me," he said. Hernandez eventually contributed $135,000 of his salary to avoid suspension. Others did likewise.

What is the Temptation?

Why have so many talented athletes chosen to use cocaine? No doubt a large part of cocaine's allure has to do with its absurd mystique as a "glamour drug" for the rich and famous. To be sure, many young men have begun to abuse cocaine long before "making it" as star athletes. Many people who use cocaine have also used drugs such as alcohol and marijuana. In fact, it is rare that an individual would use cocaine without ever having tried another drug. What does cocaine give these individuals that other drugs do not? Part of the answer lies in the effects that cocaine has on the body.

There are three main ways to ingest cocaine: snorting, injection, and smoking. Most people in this country who use cocaine ingest it through the nose; after "cutting" the cocaine powder into "lines," a user snorts the cocaine through one or both nostrils using a straw or a rolled-up piece of paper. Others inject the drug directly into the bloodstream.

Since cocaine powder cannot be smoked directly (it loses most of its effects when heated to high temperatures), a third means of ingestion is "freebasing"; a user prepares a highly purified form of the drug by "cooking" it with ether, a highly flammable liquid. The resulting powder is then smoked. The freebase procedure is extremely dangerous. Comedian Richard Pryor had a highly publicized and near-fatal accident while preparing to freebase. In addition, a new form of cocaine called "crack" has recently become popular among urban young people. Crack is a hardened, exceedingly addictive form of cocaine that, like freebase cocaine, may be smoked directly.

Dale Berra (right), son of Yogi Berra, was accused of cocaine possession and subsequently paid a fine of more than $50,000.

No matter how it is used, cocaine has powerful stimulant effects. Like caffeine, it greatly increases heart rate and blood pressure and causes a user to perspire. The pupils of the eyes become slightly dilated, and users sometimes note a change in skin temperature. The most important effect, and the reason most people use cocaine, is the euphoric feeling and the "lift" — relief from fatigue and boredom — that occurs within 30 seconds of use. These effects last less than 30 minutes, and cocaine's half-life in the bloodstream is less than one and a half hours.

Exactly why cocaine produces euphoria is not clear, although it probably has to do with the effect of the drug on the nervous system. Experts believe that cocaine affects the actions of dopamine, a neurotransmitter that helps carry messages along the central nervous system. Cocaine also blocks the body's ability to eliminate adrenaline, which may be why there is also a sudden surge in energy and well-being associated with the euphoria.

Cocaine and Athletics

Much of the world's supply of cocaine is produced in South America, and there are a large number of users in that region. Thousands of years ago, the ancient Incas of Peru chewed coca leaves, the primary source of cocaine, because the coca made it possible for them to work in the high mountains of their land for longer periods of time. In the 1880s Bolivian soldiers were given the drug to help them gain endurance and overcome fatigue. One hundred years later, as many as 90% of the natives of the Andes Mountains in Peru regularly chew coca leaves.

Cocaine increased in popularity among athletes in the early years of the 20th century. Members of the Toronto Lacrosse Club from that era, for example, reported that "the more stalwart appearing men, however, were so far used up before the match was completed that they could hardly be encouraged to finish the game, while the coca chewers were as elastic and as far from fatigue as at the commencement of the play." Many people assumed at this time that cocaine had none of the adverse side effects of other stimulants (such as amphetamines) and was not addictive like heroin.

Were they correct? In his book *Stretching the Limits* writer Lee Torrey notes that the use of cocaine in sports is

A woman sells harvested cocaine leaves on a street corner of a small Bolivian village. Nearly all of the $29 billion market for cocaine in the United States can be traced to shipments from South America.

more a prop in a "glamorous" lifestyle than a performance enhancer. "The drug's effects on strength and endurance have not been thoroughly documented," he writes. It is entirely possible that people who use cocaine feel great when they use it. They feel competent and perhaps a bit aggressive, but there is absolutely no conclusive evidence that they perform any better than they would without the drug. Perhaps the biggest reason why people, including athletes, begin using cocaine is that the drug is closely associated with wealth and prestige.

Cocaine is expensive. A single dose may be as little as a quarter of a gram (0.00875 oz.), but this amount could easily cost $25 on the street. Only the wealthy can afford a habit this expensive, and so cocaine has become known as a drug for jet setters, entertainers, and, of course, highly paid athletes. One baseball player, outfielder Lonnie Smith of the Kansas City Royals, has admitted that he used the drug from late 1979 until early 1983, when he entered a drug rehabilitation program. He estimates he spent between $50,000 and $60,000 on cocaine in that period.

Legendary ballplayer Jackie Robinson gives his son Jackie, Jr., a batting lesson. Jackie, Jr., underwent successful rehabilitation for heroin addiction but died tragically in a car accident in 1971.

The Downside

Needless to say, cocaine has its downside. In 1985 reporters Murray Chass and Michael Goodwin examined the use of cocaine in major league baseball in an article in *The New York Times*. After a three-month investigation, the reporters reached the following conclusion: "Cocaine use among baseball players has been so pervasive in recent years that the drug's debilitating effects have tarnished individual performances, shortened careers, and influenced the outcome of games and pennant races."

One of the players interviewed by the reporters was Tim Raines, a 25-year-old outfielder for the Montreal Expos. Raines told Chass and Goodwin that using cocaine hurt his performance. "I struck out a lot more; my vision was lessened. A lot of times I'd go up to the plate and the ball was right down the middle and I'd jump back, thinking it was at my head. The umpire would call it a strike and I'd start arguing. He'd say, 'That ball was right down the middle.' When you're on drugs, you don't feel you're doing anything wrong." Raines, normally an excellent base stealer, found that his skills were impaired when he was using cocaine. In 1981 he stole one out of every 2 times on base. In 1982 he stole one out of every 3.2 times.

That year Raines used the drug virtually every day and became so exhausted that he took catnaps in the dugout between innings. Sometimes he even used it during the game. "I had it in little gram bottles that I kept in my pocket," he told Chass and Goodwin. "Actually, a lot of times, I would put it in my batting glove and then in my pocket. I was trying to find ways of not getting caught." When he slid into a base, he tried to protect his investment. "Usually when I carried it in my pocket, I'd go in head first," Raines said.

The Roller Coaster of Addiction

Many people feel that they can control the amount of cocaine that they use and for that reason believe that the drug is not addictive. Research done in the 1980s, however, has shown that the drug is both psychologically and physiologically addictive.

People who regularly use cocaine find that larger and larger doses of the drug are necessary to achieve the euphoric effect. Once a user stops using cocaine, a period of depression follows. The only way to avoid the depression is by using more cocaine. This can lead to "binges" that end only when the user runs out of both cocaine and money to buy more or collapses from exhaustion. Researchers now believe that the nervous system of an addict adapts to the constant stimulation provided by cocaine use and that stopping can produce a withdrawal syndrome that is marked by an insatiable craving for the drug.

Addicts can also suffer from delirium and delusions. They may be subject to extended periods of depression and can sleep for several days following a long binge. Researchers Jacob Melamed of Northwestern University and Joseph Bleiberg of the National Rehabilitation Hospital in Washington, D.C., have also recently shown that after freebasing cocaine for an extended period, users have great difficulty in sustaining concentration and processing information. These deficits last as long as two weeks, they say. Often addicts become so preoccupied with the drug that they forget to eat correctly

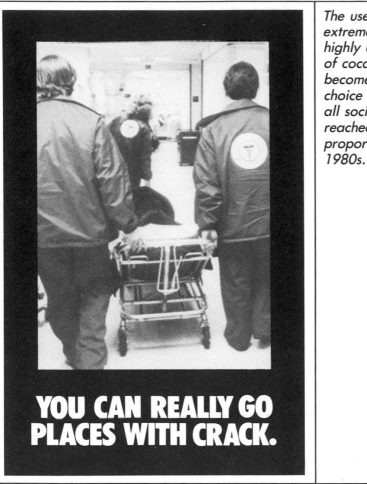

YOU CAN REALLY GO PLACES WITH CRACK.

The use of crack, an extremely addictive, highly dangerous form of cocaine that has become a drug of choice for people of all social classes, has reached epidemic proportions in the 1980s.

and wind up suffering from malnutrition, dehydration, and an unbalanced hormone system. Users who primarily snort the drug can suffer from constriction of the blood vessels in and around the nose and eventually from deterioration of the tissues. Sometimes surgery is necessary in order to correct this condition.

Overdoses from cocaine were rare until the past few years, but with more and more people freebasing and using crack, deaths from cocaine use have become all too common. One reason that cocaine, especially in purified forms, can be lethal is its recently discovered effects on the heart. Physician Henry Tazelaar of Stanford University studied the bodies of

30 cocaine users who all died in their early 30s. He found that 28 of the users had lesions (damaging changes in the tissue) on the muscle cells of the heart.

It is also possible that cocaine constricts the muscle tissue near the heart the way it affects the tissue near the nose. These lesions and constrictions in the muscle tissue of the heart can contribute to disrupting the heart's regular beat. No one really knows why an otherwise healthy heart might suddenly start beating irregularly, but the stress on it induced by cocaine is now widely recognized as extremely dangerous.

Sober Day by Day

Aside from a very few bona fide medical applications (mostly as a local anesthetic), simply possessing cocaine is a criminal offense of great severity everywhere in the United States and in most foreign countries. Even "respectable" people who use cocaine may find themselves in uncomfortable situations with people they might otherwise avoid.

Tony Elliott, a nose tackle for the New Orleans Saints of the NFL, tells a story about the day he tried to hold up his own cocaine dealer. Elliott, who earns a salary in excess of $100,000 a year, found himself short of money and desperate for cocaine. "I was shaking with fear, holding a cheap pistol behind my back," he told George Vecsey of *The New York Times*. "I didn't think he'd open the door holding a pistol, but I found myself staring at a .357 Magnum, pointed right at me. The only reason I got out of there was because he didn't see my pistol." Elliott, who now spends most of the off-season counseling kids with drug problems, says he has been sober for "two years and three months—day by day."

Tommy Simpson takes the lead in the Tour de France race of 1962. Five years later, Simpson died while competing in the same race. Traces of amphetamines were subsequently found in his blood.

CHAPTER 3

ERGOGENIC DRUGS

In contrast to recreational drugs, which are used, in general, simply to get high, ergogenic or performance-enhancing drugs are used by athletes primarily to help them perform faster, stronger, and longer. In contrast to what most athletes (and quite a few trainers and coaches) believe, however, the evidence that these drugs actually help athletes is sketchy at best. Despite the lack of clear proof, many athletes believe that these drugs help them and continue to use them even though they are aware that they pose grave health dangers.

Amphetamines

There are actually many different amphetamines — a short-hand word for a(lpha) m(ethyl) ph(enyl) et(hyl) amine. Benzedrine, Dexedrine, Didrex, Preludin, Phenzine, Plegine, Ritalin, Tenuate, and Pre-Sate are all similar drugs with slightly different chemical structures. First chemically synthesized in 1887, amphetamines belong to a class of drugs known as sympathomimetics, because they have many of the same properties in the body as the natural stimulant adrenaline. They act mostly on the central nervous system and sympathetic nervous system (responsible for regulating many of the body's unconscious processes).

San Francisco 49er Ronnie Lott (right) collides with Mark Clayton of the Miami Dolphins during the 1985 Super Bowl, exhibiting the healthy, natural aggression that is characteristic of football. Most athletes avoid amphetamines precisely because these drugs can precipitate dangerously violent reactions to competition.

One of the first groups of people to use amphetamines regularly were members of the American armed forces during World War II. GIs found the pills in their standard-issue kits. Although the pills were intended to enhance their battle endurance, the GIs began using them to improve their performance in recreational football games. In later years use of these stimulants spread to include some professional sports figures. In 1958 the American College of Sports Medicine estimated that 35% of NFL trainers, coaches, and assistants had had personal contact with amphetamines. Another study reported that almost a quarter of all college athletes had used a stimulant such as an amphetamine at least once before a game or meet.

Amphetamine use among athletes did not became rampant, however, until the 1960s. By all accounts the 1960 Olympics marked a nadir in the history of drug use in international sport. At the time there were no rules against using stimulants to help performance. On opening day, Danish cyclist Knud Jensen collapsed during the time trials for the 100-kilometer team race. Jensen, who was 23, later died of what was officially called "sunstroke." An autopsy, however, showed large amounts of amphetamine and other drugs in his bloodstream. Several of Jensen's teammates were also taken to the hospital, all with symptoms of mild sunstroke. Later, at the 1967 Pan American Games in Winnipeg, Canada, seven cyclists were found to have amphetamines in their urine. Also in 1967, 29-year-old cyclist Tommy Simpson died during the famed Tour de France race, and amphetamines and methylamphetamines were found in his blood.

In this country, amphetamine abuse in sports continued unabated. In 1972 one researcher reported that 74 of 93 NFL players interviewed took amphetamines regularly. He reported that amphetamines might help such athletes by giving them more energy and increasing their confidence and aggressiveness. Of course, athletes are not the only ones to abuse amphetamines. Truck drivers needing to stay awake over long hauls and students trying to study for long periods have both been known to turn to amphetamines, and there is a hard-core group of users who simply enjoy the euphoria of "speeding." Such speed "freaks" sometimes inject the drug instead of (or in addition to) taking it orally.

Cleveland Indians pitcher Sam McDowell slides into third base in a 1964 game. Athletic maneuvers such as this require coordination and timing, skills heavy amphetamine abuse may diminish.

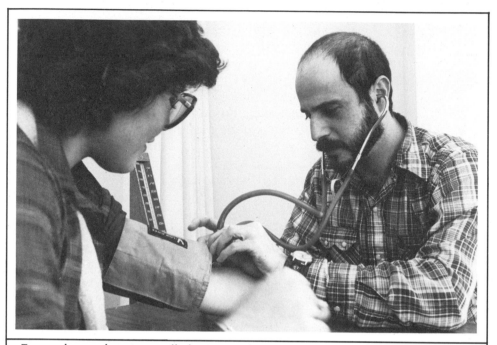

Even when taken in small doses amphetamines can cause high blood pressure, a chronic condition that often leads to serious ailments such as stroke and heart disease.

Short-Term and Long-Term Effects

When taken in relatively low doses amphetamines cause increases in breathing and heart rate. Blood pressure rises and the appetite is suppressed. Users also feel euphoric, and some feel as if they are floating. Reflexes are heightened, and the limbs and hands may tremble slightly. Amphetamines also dull feelings of pain. At higher doses, users can feel flushed, or they may appear pallid. The heartbeat becomes irregular, and the tremors can increase and become incapacitating. Finally, a user can collapse.

The long-term effects of amphetamine use should probably be enough to convince anyone to stay away from them. People who use amphetamines regularly over a period of months often become irritable and indecisive. They are prone to headaches, do not sleep well, and frequently suffer from dangerous dietary deficiencies. Heart problems can develop, including high blood pressure and irregular heartbeat. Tolerance also occurs in regular users, meaning that greater amounts of the drug are necessary to produce the desired effect.

Although it has never been proved that the drugs are physically addictive, enough people have found it difficult to quit using them that they are usually referred to as psychologically addictive. Indeed, the craving for amphetamines can be immense. For example, animals that become accustomed to using these drugs will keep trying to get more of them for twice as long as will animals that are addicted to heroin.

Fatalities from amphetamine use are rare but possible. The chance of death increases if amphetamines are mixed with another drug such as alcohol or if an athlete combines these drugs with overexertion. The deaths of Knud Jensen and U.S. track star Dick Howard, another participant in the 1960 Olympics, resulted from this mixture of amphetamines and heat exhaustion.

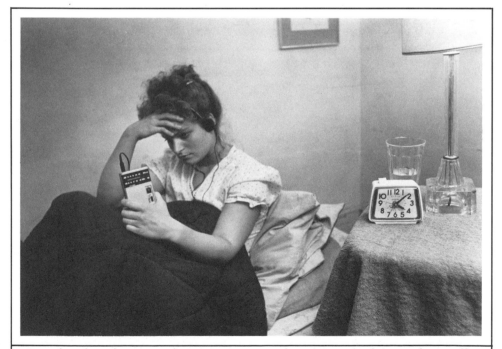

People who abuse amphetamines over a long period of time often suffer from insomnia or chronic sleeplessness, which in turn can trigger such unpleasant effects as irritability and headaches.

Amphetamines and Athletics

One of the earliest researchers to study scientifically the effects of amphetamines on athletes was Henry Beecher, who in 1959 showed that a dose of between 14 and 21 mg for every 70 kg of body weight taken 2–3 hours before an event improved the speed of runners and swimmers and the performance of weight throwers in 75% of the athletes he studied. These findings were partially responsible for the vast amount of amphetamine abuse among athletes in the early 1960s.

In 1980 physician Joseph Chandler reported that a dose of 15 mg of dexedrine for every 70 kg of body weight increased the duration, acceleration, and knee-extension strength in runners. Interestingly, Chandler found that top speed was not increased. Recently, however, the beneficial effects of amphetamines have begun to be called into question. Exercise physiologist Lawrence Golding studied 10 members of Kent State's track team and 10 nonathletes. He asked them to run on a treadmill until they were exhausted.

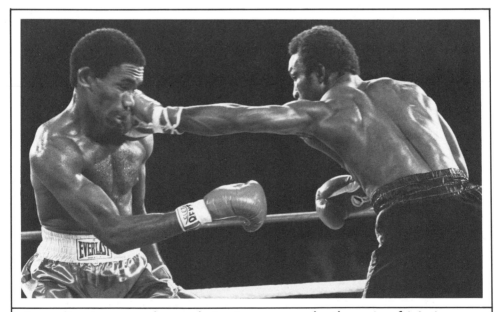

According to research, amphetamines may make the pain of injuries suffered in such sports as boxing more tolerable, but athletes pay for this analgesic effect by taking much longer to recover.

Some of the runners were given amphetamines before the test, others were given placebos — sugar pills that looked like the amphetamines. Although the runners who were given the amphetamines tended to run slightly longer than those who were given placebos, the differences were so small that Golding could not conclude that the drug had had a significant impact.

Twelve minutes after completing their first run, Golding asked the runners to get back on the treadmill. This time, those who were given the drug could not run as long as those who had been given sugar. Again, the differences were not very substantial, but the direction in which they point is significant. Amphetamines may make pain more tolerable, but athletes pay for this analgesic effect by taking much longer to recover. Recovery time for runners may be as much as doubled, and football players who use amphetamines are, not infrequently, relatively slow to recover from bruises.

Many authorities believe that high doses of amphetamines lead to uncharacteristic behavior changes in athletes. Abuse of amphetamines may lead to profuse sweating, violent vomiting, and diarrhea. Otherwise calm individuals may become easily enraged. Many observers feel, in fact, that the use of amphetamines may be one cause of the recent increase of violence in professional sports.

Steroids

In March 1986 Michael David Williams, a 26-year-old enlisted man in the U.S. Navy with eight years of solid service, went on trial, accused of a crime spree in June 1985 that included robbery and arson. In his defense, Williams's attorneys alleged that their client, an amateur weight lifter, had used drugs regularly for months and that immediately preceding the rampage he had dramatically increased the dosage. Testifying at the trial in Upper Marlboro, Maryland, psychiatrist Michael Spodak contended that the drugs altered Williams's personality, causing him to become aggressive and hostile.

Williams was eventually found guilty but not criminally responsible by Judge Audrey Melbourne. In her decision, she noted that at the time of the break-ins Williams was "suffering from an organic personality syndrome caused by toxic levels of anabolic steroids taken to enhance his ability to win the body-building contests."

Anabolic steroids — synthetic compounds formulated to act like the male sex hormone testosterone — are the subject of much discussion these days. Many athletes, including male and female bodybuilders, weight lifters, runners, swimmers, and football players, have used them because they believe, perhaps mistakenly, that in doing so they will gain size and strength advantages in their sports.

In the body of a man, testosterone is secreted by the Leydig cells in the testes. It has two main functions: androgenic and anabolic. Androgenic effects are those that relate to the development of male sex characteristics. Anabolic effects are those that relate to the development of muscle tissue. During puberty testosterone normally functions both to produce secondary sex characteristics, such as body hair, enlarged larynx, and a deep voice in young men, and to increase body size. The half-life of the substance is extremely short.

In order to produce a drug to treat those who suffer from a natural lack of testosterone, pharmacologists learned to alter one form of testosterone slightly, greatly increasing the length of time that the drug is active. Testosterone was first isolated in 1935, and soon similar forms with names such as Dianabol, Durabolin, Deca-Durabolin, and Winstrol were produced. But what do these drugs actually do?

One of the main effects of anabolic steroids is to increase the production of red blood cells and muscle tissue without producing much of the androgenic effects of testosterone itself. At present, there are only four legal uses for the drugs. Physicians prescribe them in the treatment of certain forms of anemia, certain kinds of cancers, pituitary dwarfism, and serious hormone disturbances.

There are two principal forms of anabolic steroids: those that are taken orally and those that are injected. The immediate effects of both kinds include mood swings of many different sorts. In one study, physicians Ian Wilson, Arthur Prange, Jr., and Patricio Lara found that four out of five men who were given a steroid while suffering from depression experienced delusions. A research team from Great Britain found that a patient who was given steroids became progressively dizzy, disoriented, and incoherent. In addition, physicians William Annitto and William Layman have described a case of a young man who was diagnosed as schizophrenic after he, unbeknownst to his physicians, took steroids to help with his weight lifting. After taking the drugs, the young man suffered severe depression and anxiety and had difficulty sleeping.

Although many people who use them do not suffer side effects this severe, anabolic steroids produce changes in the electroencephalogram (an image of brain electrical activity) very similar to those produced by stimulant drugs such as amphetamines. Some researchers believe that these changes may be responsible for some of the more common changes in behavior seen in users of steroids, such as increased hostility and aggressiveness.

Even though anabolic steroids have been specifically designed to reproduce few of the masculinizing effects of testosterone, some inevitably remain. Men and women who use them sometimes develop acne, a deepened voice, and abnormal hair growth, conditions that are not necessarily reversible. Men who use steroids sometimes have changes in their sexual-arousal patterns and may become more or less interested in sex.

The Dangers of Anabolic Steroids

In its stand on the use of anabolic steroids by athletes, the ACSM documents three main physical problems associated with long-term use: adverse effects on the liver, the cardiovascular system, and reproductive system.

The most serious effect of anabolic steroids on the liver is known as peliosis hepatis — blood-filled cysts in the liver. If these cysts rupture, they can cause liver failure, which can result in death. There is some evidence, however, that once the drug is stopped, the cysts may become smaller or disappear. The use of steroids has also been associated with cancerous tumors of the liver, some of which are reduced when the drugs are discontinued. Steroids may also interfere with the flow of bile produced in the liver, resulting in a condition known as intrahepatic cholestasis. There is also some evidence that the use of steroids is linked to increased risk of developing gallstones.

Although the effects of anabolic steroids on the cardiovascular system vary according to the individual taking these drugs, all of the effects are potentially hazardous to health.

Oklahoma linebacker Brian Bosworth was prohibited from participating in the 1987 Orange Bowl when traces of steroids prescribed to him for an injury were found in his blood.

For example, there are two kinds of cholesterol: high-density lipoprotein cholesterol (HDL) and low-density lipoprotein cholesterol (LDL). Researchers now regard HDL as of beneficial value to the body and LDL as potentially dangerous. Using anabolic steroids tends to lower the level of HDL in most people. Perhaps because of changes in the levels of HDL and LDL, use of steroids also puts users at a higher risk of developing high blood pressure and blood-clotting problems. Some physicians claim that steroids also cause abnormal fat deposits to develop and alter the way the body processes carbohydrates.

Men who use anabolic steroids face the possibility of serious reproductive problems. In addition to the masculinizing problems mentioned earlier, the drugs lower the amount of sperm in the semen, which may make conception difficult or impossible. The testes decrease in size, and the amount of natural testosterone and other hormones that nourish them also decreases. In some men, the prostate gland becomes enlarged. A recent report in the medical journal *The Lancet* noted that one 40-year-old man developed prostate cancer, perhaps related to his 18 years of using anabolic steroids. Most of the symptoms of drug use go away after steroids are discontinued, but others, such as the development of abnormal tissue in the liver, testes, and prostate gland, may not.

The effects of anabolic steroids on women can be startling and dramatic. In addition to the masculinizing effects, the drugs reduce the levels of female hormones, such as estrogen and progesterone — both of which are crucial to the healthy functioning of a woman's menstrual cycle. Some women stop menstruating completely, while others find that their periods are irregular or of a different duration than usual.

One of the most devastating effects of steroid use happens exclusively to young people. Steroids cause the premature closure of the space between parts of the body's long bones. This process, which usually takes place during adolescence, may continue in healthy people until the age of 18 and beyond. In teenagers who use steroids, this process can be artificially accelerated, and growth may be irreversibly stunted.

Use of steroids increases appetite, mental intensity, energy, and tolerance of pain. It is also associated with drastic sleep disturbances, including frequent nightmares. The adverse effect of steroids may linger for weeks and months after the drugs are discontinued. People who have become accustomed to anabolic steroids may feel depressed and listless when they give up the drugs. They sometimes feel less confident in themselves and may be slow to return to normal sleep patterns and energy level.

Use of Steroids Among Athletes

Steroids not only cause unwanted, often dangerous side effects but are prohibited in international competition and in many national competitions as well. Given all of the dangers, why might top athletes — amateurs as well as professionals — resort to steroids?

The pressures of national and international competition are enormous. The drive to excel and win sometimes becomes so overwhelming that an athlete might do anything to obtain a slight advantage. According to journalist and former weight lifter Terry Todd, athletes first began to use the drugs in 1954 when physician John Ziegler, team physician for the U.S. weight lifting team, accompanied the team to the world championships in Vienna, Austria. There Ziegler says he met the Russian team doctor, who told him that the Russian athletes, who seemed to be invincible in the competition, were using testosterone.

Ziegler brought the news back to the United States, and soon virtually every competitive weight lifter was using testosterone and then anabolic steroids. Thirty years later, some sources claim that the drugs have been used by four out of five international weight lifters and those who participate in field events such as the shot put, the discus, the javelin, and the hammer throw. Edwin Moses, the world record holder in the 110-meter hurdle, believes that half of the top track-and-field performers have used them. There is evidence that these drugs are still being used. At least five athletes were disqualified from the Los Angeles Olympics in 1984 when tests showed they had used anabolic steroids. The Japanese masseur Yoshitaka Yahagi has been banned from Olympic competition through 1992 for giving a banned drug to a volleyball player who suffered from a cold at the games, telling him that it was an herbal product. Steroid use has also been reported among both college and professional football players. Brian Bosworth, All-American linebacker from the University of Oklahoma, was prohibited from playing in the 1987 Orange Bowl after testing positive for steroid use.

As mentioned earlier, there are only four legal uses for steroids, yet sources estimate that only 20–30% of the steroids produced are used for these purposes. A 1981 study of elite athletes who admitted using anabolic steroids found that 36% of those who used them got them from physicians, 10% from trainers, and 9% from pharmacists. An overwhelming 45% said they bought the drugs illegally. Duncan MacDougall, professor in the departments of physical education and medicine at McMaster University in Hamilton, Ontario, believes that anabolic steroids are relatively easy to obtain. In an article published in 1983, he wrote, "I would suggest that you can go into almost any major body-building club in any city in Canada and within two hours have a month's or six month's supply of steroids at prices that are actually lower than a pharmacist's." There are reports of children as young as 12 years old buying the drugs in gyms and using them.

Many athletes believe that using steroids while training results in greater gains in strength and body size than does training alone. On this point, the evidence from the scientific literature is contradictory and inconclusive. One of the behavior changes seen in those who use steroids is increased aggressiveness and hostility. As far as strength is concerned, the ACSM states that "the use of anabolic-androgenic steroids, especially by experienced weight trainers, can often increase strength gains beyond those seen with training and diet alone. This positive effect is usually small and obviously is not exhibited by all individuals." Some researchers, however, think that the feelings of aggression and hostility cause the athlete to train harder, which of course would result in bigger muscles and larger strength gains.

Similarly, the evidence on body-size increases is difficult to interpret. Some studies with humans and animals show that athletes who take steroids while they train show larger weight gains than those who only train. But other studies, in which the athletes do not know whether they are ingesting steroids or simply sugar pills (placebos), show inconclusive results.

Part of the body-size controversy centers on determining the type of tissue growth that the drugs promote. Everyone agrees that those who use anabolic steroids gain weight. But although some experts think that the increases are in real muscle tissue, others say that the tissue is abnormal and that the weight gain is partly due to water retained in the body. The ACSM position paper on this subject notes that "anabolic-androgenic steroids can contribute to an increase in body weight in the lean mass compartment of the body. The amount of weight gained in the training studies has been small but statistically significant." Of course, some athletes can ill afford to gain weight. For example, wrestlers who have used anabolic steroids to help with muscular growth find that they add weight that is unwanted and difficult to lose.

It would be easier to monitor steroid use if they were always used under a physician's supervision, but this seldom

Dr. Jonathan S. Dixon (left) and Dr. C. H. Li were members of a research team that discovered the chemical composition of human growth hormone (hgh). The chart they are holding illustrates the code words that represent the configuration of amino acids in hgh.

occurs. Whereas most of the successful experiments with strength and weight gains have been done under carefully controlled conditions of diet and training, the vast majority of steroid users regulate their own intake of the drugs. The normal male produces about 10 mg of testosterone each day. Some athletes who abuse steroids have been known to use doses of 200 or 300 mg each day.

Human Growth Hormone

One of the newest and potentially most dangerous developments in the race to perfect strength-building drugs is synthetic production of human growth hormone. This hormone, which is produced naturally in extremely limited quantities in the pituitary gland, regulates children's body growth. In the last few years scientists have determined how to produce the drug in large quantities so that children whose bodies do not produce enough of the drug naturally and therefore would otherwise be abnormally short in stature might grow normally.

As physician William Taylor and others have pointed out, however, there is a danger that in the future this drug may be abused by unscrupulous parents, trainers, and coaches who seek to accelerate artificially the growth of children in their care. Taylor thinks that national and international authorities ought to be on the lookout for people who try to produce artificial "super athletes" by administering this drug. Physician Robert Kerr, who claims to supervise 10,000 individuals using steroids, believes that human growth hormone is "an elite drug in track and field competition today." The substance has not yet been banned by any major sports authority.

Taylor warns that at least two other natural hormones are also close to being commercially mass-produced by chemical laboratories: growth hormone releasing factor and somatomedin-C, both of which can affect the normal growth process. Until the full effects of human growth hormone, growth hormone releasing factor, and somatomedin C on young people are known, they remain large, troubling question marks in the future of sports.

Not all athletes are ready to use whatever artificial means are necessary to win. Physician Bob Goldman, chairman of the Sports Medicine Committee of the Amateur Athletic Union (AAU) and an avid fitness buff, has since 1975 played a major role in the campaign to eliminate the use of steroids in sports. In his 1984 book *Death in the Locker Room: Steroids and Sports* Goldman forcefully argues that athletes can and do win without the help of ergogenic drugs. Goldman ought to know. As holder of the world records in handstand push-ups (321) and consecutive sit-ups (more than 13,500), he has never used drugs, and he urges others not to. Goldman believes that there is greater emphasis today than ever before on "natural competitions," where none of the athletes have used ergogenic drugs to help them train. "At least I hope this is the trend," he says, "or else sports contests of the future will be between doctors and the pills they prescribe instead of between athletes."

As more and more athletes are publicly acknowledging the folly of using steroids, it is becoming easier to see how athletes of the future might avoid them. Bill Fralic, an offensive lineman for the Atlanta Falcons of the NFL (which prohibits the use of steroids but had not tested for them as of the end of the 1986–87 season), used steroids as an undergraduate at the University of Pittsburgh because weight lifting and steroids were important parts of training for college football players. Why did he stop? "I finally realized that it doesn't make you more of a man to say that you can lift more weight than the next guy," he says.

Rod Dixon expresses fatigue and exhilaration after winning the New York City Marathon in 1983. The body's natural opiates induce a state of euphoria in many long-distance athletes known as "runner's high."

CHAPTER 4

THERAPEUTIC DRUGS

Increasingly, top athletes look to science for ways to speed recovery time, heal injuries, and reduce pain. One of the most potent means is through therapeutic drugs. This chapter will discuss the use of three types of these drugs. The first and most important are the painkillers — drugs used to reduce the sensations of pain and allow athletes to continue playing even though they may be injured. The second group is the antianxiety drugs — those modern drugs that are used to calm the nerves of those who compete. A third category of drugs considered is the diuretics; normally prescribed to help remove unwanted water from the body, these drugs are used by some athletes to help lower body weight quickly. All three of these drug types are used widely by professional and amateur athletes, although not all athletes are fully aware of the risks they pose to health. In contrast to recreational and ergogenic drugs, there are perfectly legitimate medical reasons for using therapeutic drugs under some circumstances. These substances, however, are not without their risks and should always be used carefully and under the supervision of a physician.

Painkillers

In April 1978 basketball star Bill Walton was playing in the NBA playoffs when he began to feel an intense pain in his left foot. Walton had suffered a series of injuries to the foot

Bill Walton (playing here with the San Diego Clippers) suffered a foot injury during his career with the Portland Trail Blazers but was given painkillers and urged to continue playing. The short-term solution resulted in a broken foot that kept him from competing for a year.

that had left it in a weakened condition. The team physician for the Portland Trail Blazers, Robert Cook, injected Walton with a painkiller that allowed him to keep playing a few minutes longer. Walton returned to the game but had to come out after several minutes when the pain became unbearable. Later, X rays showed that he had suffered a broken bone after the injection. The injury meant a year on the sidelines for Walton and came close to ending his career. Indeed, complications arising from the injury were to keep Walton from completing an entire season until 1985. Walton contended that Cook's injection had indirectly caused the broken bone by allowing him to play when his initial injury indicated that he should have been sidelined. Experts agree that the injection, which was given with the player's consent, may have contributed to the broken bone.

Pain serves a valuable function to human beings by providing a warning that something is wrong. The immediate response of the body to pain is similar to its response in cases of great fear. When the body feels pain, we cry out, move away from the source of pain, and experience changes in blood pressure and in the electrical properties of the skin. When an athlete is injured, the pain translates into a simple message: "Stop playing or you will hurt yourself worse!"

Exactly how the body feels "pain" is not clearly understood. What is known, however, is that certain classes of drugs are able to blunt the body's ability to feel pain. There are three main classes of these drugs: local anesthetics, anti-inflammatory drugs, and narcotic analgesics.

When a basketball player sprains an ankle (stretches or tears one of the ligaments in the ankle) or a football player strains a muscle in his thigh (stretches or tears the muscle-tendon link), simply applying a cold compress often helps alleviate the pain. In the past trainers used sponges soaked in ice water. In the 1980s they often use aerosol sprays — which evaporate very quickly and remove excess heat — to accomplish the same thing. Both methods temporarily cool the skin and provide short-term relief.

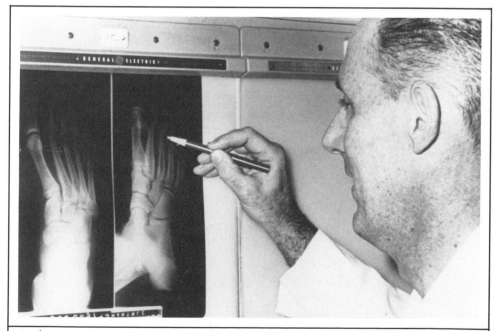

A doctor examines an X ray of Mickey Mantle's fractured foot. Anesthetic drugs may alleviate certain pains for a short while, but long-term problems can develop without proper medical attention.

Sometimes trainers try to allow athletes to compete even if the players feel pain before a game starts. To do this, they sometimes resort to injecting the player with anesthetic drugs such as Novocain and Xylocaine. These drugs, which are injected directly into an injured joint or muscle, temporarily block the body's feeling of pain in the specific area in which they are injected, but they can be dangerous. In large doses they can cause convulsions and death.

Anti-inflammatory Drugs

For more prolonged control of pain, athletes and trainers often turn to anti-inflammatory drugs. When a part of the body is damaged, the cells nearby produce hormones called prostaglandins. Among other effects, these hormones cause inflammation around the site of the wound by dilating (or enlarging) the small blood vessels nearest it. The area quickly becomes red, puffy, and swollen with fluid. Prostaglandins also activate nerve cells nearby and so increase feelings of pain.

There are several substances that can halt the action of prostaglandins. One of the most important of these agents is acetylsalicylic acid, or aspirin. When taken in moderate doses, aspirin stops the production of prostaglandins very effectively, but if taken in larger doses, it can produce discomfort in the stomach and intestines.

Another common anti-inflammatory agent is called phenylbutazone, or "bute." This drug is more powerful than aspirin and is somewhat more popular among athletes. The side effects of both aspirin and phenylbutazone include diarrhea, dizziness, headaches, and retention of water. Prolonged use of "bute" and related drugs can result in anemia and ulcers of the stomach or intestines.

The strongest class of the anti-inflammatory drugs is the corticosteroids. Related to the anabolic steroids (see Chapter 3) in chemical makeup, they are synthetic derivatives of similar substances found in the body and are used principally to ease joint pain.

During the stress of exercise, the top layer (or cortex) of the adrenal glands produces these hormones, which are divided into two main groups: the glucocorticoids, which suppress inflammation, and the mineralocorticoids, which control the action of the kidneys. Corticosteroids have euphoric effects, and there are reports of athletes who take them to get "high" as well as to relieve the pain of an overused joint. Corticosteroids are used infrequently today, but for some years they were the drug of choice for treating "tennis elbow," for example. We now know that corticosteroids are not nearly as safe to use as once thought; taking these drugs may lead to severe hormone problems once the drug supply is stopped. People who have used corticosteroids are often unable to fight off infection. In women the drugs may cause abnormal hair growth and menstrual difficulties.

It is also possible that using the drugs actually weakens the joint to which they are applied and makes it more difficult for an injury to the joint to heal. One research team found that if the steroid cortisone (a corticosteroid) was injected into a normal tendon in animals, that tendon would be weakened for up to two weeks. Considering the fact that most athletes use corticosteroids immediately before competition, one might guess that the risk of reinjury would be quite high. In her book *Sports Medicine for the Female Athlete*, physician Christine Haycock warns that collagen, the principal component of connective tissue, may be damaged by repeated injections of a corticosteroid such as cortisone. "The possibility of arthritis in later life from repeated injuries [caused by the use of anti-inflammatory agents] should be of real concern to everyone involved in athletic activities," she says.

Narcotic Analgesics

The third category of painkillers is known as narcotic analgesics — painkillers derived from opium — morphine, heroin, and codeine. In contemporary society everyone knows that morphine and heroin, which can be smoked, eaten, or injected, are highly addictive, both psychologically and physiologically. Use of the drugs can cause vomiting and diarrhea, and withdrawal from their use needs to be carefully monitored by a physician. Codeine, on the other hand, is relatively nonaddictive and may be permitted, under some circumstances, for therapeutic use in athletes.

The narcotic analgesics are also potent painkillers and have been used (at least in the past) by athletes to dull extreme pain. They work through the central nervous system,

A Thai tribesman examines an opium plant prior to harvest. Some narcotic analgesics, which are derived from the opium poppy, are used legitimately by athletes for therapeutic purposes.

initially producing a stimulant effect and then a dulling of pain throughout the body. Narcotics seem to work by acting upon those parts of the brain and central nervous system receptive to a recently discovered group of compounds called "endorphins." These substances, which occur naturally in the body, are the brain's natural opiates and are intricately connected to the body's pain-sensing mechanism. Parts of the central nervous system, including regions in the brain and in the spinal column, seem especially sensitive to endorphins, and, by extension, to narcotic drugs.

Endocrinologist David Carr conducted research on these natural opiates by measuring the amount of endorphins present in his subjects before and after they rode a stationary bicycle for an hour. In each person, he found increased levels of endorphins after biking. Some researchers have even theorized that endorphins might be the substances that produce "runner's high," a mysterious state of euphoria some runners say they experience after running long distances.

Although it is unlikely that the endorphin story is quite that simple, it is possible that narcotics such as morphine and heroin actually fool the body into thinking that they are endorphins, thereby affecting the sensation of pain. Perhaps as we gain a greater understanding of the body's own pain-regulating system (including the endorphins), we will be able to harness the power of our "internal narcotics" to dull pain.

In all of the confusion about painkillers and advanced research, one troublesome question remains: "Why should an athlete be forced to play with pain?" As mentioned earlier, when Bill Walton left the 1978 playoff game with a broken foot, a few uninformed fans found reason to question his strength of character despite the fact that he was in obvious pain. As fans, parents, coaches, trainers, and teammates, we expect a great deal from athletic superstars. Of course, in many cases the athletes are paid a great deal to do what we expect them to. But the demands we place on them may at

A member of the Chinese women's basketball team trains for the 1984 Olympic Games. Injuries sustained in this sort of rugged training can often be effectively treated with anti-inflammatory drugs.

times be too high. Our demand for superhuman feats and indifference to bodily pain from professional athletes begins in the values that we teach at the college and high school level. We need to ask ourselves if we are expecting too much from athletes.

Antianxiety Drugs

Athletes may sometimes seem superhuman, but even those who compete at the international level have weaknesses; even the best occasionally suffer from "nerves." When their own abilities are not enough to keep them calm before a game or meet, some turn to drugs. In one study of college football players, 11% indicated that they had used some sort of antianxiety medication.

The antianxiety drugs used by athletes come in two varieties — benzodiazepines and beta-blockers. Minor tranquilizers such as benzodiazepines have been prescribed by physicians for years to treat minor depression, tension, and anxiety. Usually given in oral doses of between 5 mg and 25 mg, drugs such as Valium, Librium, Serax, Tranxene, and Dalmane are absorbed in the intestinal tract and quickly act as depressants on the limbic system — the center of emotions in the brain.

It is said that many sports are as much mental as they are physical. This may be especially true of individual sports such as shooting, archery, and golf, which rely on powers of concentration. These are sports in which strength and power are not nearly as important as control and precision. They are also the sports in which benzodiazepine abuse has surfaced. Athletes in these sports claim that moderate levels of these drugs allow them to perform flawlessly, with their nerves and emotions in check.

Actually, some people who use these drugs become intoxicated, and their mental state resembles alcoholic drunkenness. Like alcoholics, benzodiazepine users may not be aware of their reduced psychomotor abilities. The studies are generally inconclusive in this area, but many show impaired psychomotor abilities for those who take these drugs. For example, one 1979 study found that those who take minor sedatives are at four times the risk of having an automobile accident as those who do not take the drugs.

Two archers show the concentration, control, and precision needed to excel. Some athletes in this sport claim that moderate levels of benzodiazepines enhance their abilities in competition.

There is also a small but significant risk that a person will react strongly to the drug in an unexpected way; a minority of those who take benzodiazepines are at risk of becoming overly excited, enraged, and hostile, especially if they also drink.

There is also the risk of addiction. Although it would be difficult to accomplish, taking 300–600 mg a day for several weeks produces an addiction to benzodiazepines, complete with withdrawal symptoms that can include seizures. There are scattered reports of individuals becoming dependent on far lower doses, especially if they are taken over a period of time. When people finally stop taking benzodiazepines, they usually lose weight, have headaches, and feel changes in their ability to see, hear, and feel.

Although the dangers of these drugs are not completely clear, prudent athletes should steer clear of benzodiazepines unless prescribed by a physician, for no other reason than that research on the subject is incomplete. Very little is known, for example, about the effects of tranquilizers on strength or endurance. At least some of these questions are likely to have unpleasant answers.

Beta-Blockers

The other class of antianxiety drugs used by athletes are the beta-blockers. These drugs, including Nifedipine, Inderal, Eraldin, and Sotacor, are widely used to treat high blood pressure and certain heart conditions, with great success. One of the body's immediate reactions during stress is to increase blood pressure. This happens because the hormone adrenaline, which is produced during stress, activates certain sites on the tissue of the heart called beta-receptors. Beta-blockers, on the other hand, stop the adrenaline from binding to these receptors and block part of adrenaline's effect.

As is the case with the benzodiazepines, there are some people who believe that beta-blockers allow athletes to perform calmly with little risk to their health. Pistol shooters, ski jumpers, and archers are known to have experimented with the drugs, as have participants in combination sports such as the modern pentathlon (which includes shooting) and biathlon (shooting and cross-country skiing). A 1985 article in the scientific journal *Sports Medicine* concluded that the "ability to perform athletic events requiring high levels of motor control under emotional stress but not high levels of aerobic or anaerobic energy release is probably increased during beta-blockade."

But the list of side effects and effects of unknown consequence might discourage some of those who are excited by these early conclusions. Beta-blockers interfere, as one might expect, with the entire endocrine system. Since they affect the action of adrenaline, the hormone system can be shifted ever so slightly out of balance, blocking the effect of noradrenaline and human growth hormone. The drugs reduce liver function and the production of a liver enzyme necessary for proper elimination of body wastes.

For other athletes, the effects of taking beta-blockers might, in fact, be counterproductive. Muscle strength seems not to be affected, but aerobic power, endurance, and short, explosive muscular exercise all reportedly suffer. In fact, many athletes who have tried beta-blockers complain of muscular fatigue.

Under the direction of a physician, beta-blockers have potentially important applications in sports, particularly for those with high blood pressure and cardiovascular problems. So far, however, they have proved difficult to regulate. Until they are, uncontrolled and hazardous experimentation by athletes will probably continue. The irony is that these drugs, which hold such promise in the treatment of heart disease and high blood pressure, may cause damage in as yet unknown ways to athletes who use them.

Diuretics

Anyone who knows high school or college wrestlers would never invite them to dinner the night before a meet. Life between competitions for wrestlers, as well as for certain other athletes (such as boxers and jockeys), involves a constant battle to lose weight, including starvation diets, profuse sweating, and liquid deprivation. Historically, at least, that effort has included diuretics, which are drugs specifically designed to help individuals eliminate liquid from the body.

Under the direction of a physician, diuretics such as trichlormethiazide, methyclothiazide, and bumetanide increase urine flow and are used as a dieting aid or to help women who feel bloated just before menstruation.

Typically, wrestlers who take diuretics ingest the drug just prior to weighing in; their aim is to lose weight in order to make a lower weight class. After weighing in, they drink a huge amount of water to replace the fluid they have lost.

Virtually every study concerning the use of diuretics in sports shows that the urinating-drinking technique is a bad idea. This process dramatically alters the body's balance of electrolytes (substances in body fluids capable of carrying electrical charges) and can have detrimental effects on the functioning of the kidneys. There is decreased blood flow to the kidneys, and the amount of fluid being filtered by the kidneys is also lower. Muscular strength and work performance are both decreased. Most important, there are significant negative effects on the performance of the heart — the rate is increased, while total output is decreased.

Two wrestlers compete in the 1984 Olympics. Some wrestlers have attempted to keep their weight down by taking diuretics, but these drugs alter body chemistry and can damage the kidneys.

The ACSM has made a strong stand on the use of drastic weight loss strategies by wrestlers, including the use of diuretics: "The goal of an effective weight loss regimen is not merely to lose weight. Weight control requires a lifelong commitment, an understanding of eating habits and a willingness to change them. Frequent exercise is also necessary. . . . Crash dieting and other promised weight loss cures are ineffective."

Another troublesome use of diuretics has emerged over the past few years. Some athletes who fear testing positive for banned substances (see Chapter 5) try to flush out their systems by taking diuretics and eliminating the drugs more quickly through urination. This method does not work, and competitors who try it may find that they have only added to their problems — athletes can be disqualified from competition as easily for using diuretics as they can for taking other banned substances. Of course, the same health hazards, including damage to the kidneys and the body's electrolyte balance, apply to those who use diuretics to remove prohibited substances.

In 1986 both the National Football League Players' Association and NFL Commissioner Pete Rozelle (right) proposed plans to institute stringent drug-testing procedures for football players.

CHAPTER 5

DRUG TESTING

Most people agree that it would be difficult, if not impossible, to eliminate drugs completely from sports, but that does not mean that organized sports associations are ignoring the dangers of drugs. The main weapon that these associations possess to protect the health of those who participate in sports, as well as ensure that competitions are fair and natural, is drug testing.

Technologically, the drug-testing arsenal is extremely powerful. Rules and methods of testing vary from organization to organization, but the means for discovering whether an athlete has used a prohibited substance are more discerning than ever. For the most part, testing for drug use centers on the ergogenic and recreational drugs. Among the substances for which athletes are most commonly tested are amphetamines, steroids, marijuana, cocaine, and narcotics. Less frequently, authorities look for painkillers and antianxiety drugs, alcohol, and caffeine.

Overall, the clamor for testing in sports is growing on all levels. Testing is routine in international and Olympic competition. If the labor issues can be ironed out, it may well become the rule in professional sports in this country. Even at the collegiate level, more and more voices in favor of testing are being heard.

Physicians Bert Zairns, John Bergfeld, and Bob Leach are all strongly in favor of mandatory testing. At the 1986 annual meeting of the American Academy of Orthopedic Surgeons, Zairns, who is the team physician for the New England Patriots of the NFL, was critical of those athletes seeking to block drug testing. All three physicians were interviewed in *American Medical News*, and Zairns commented, "I find it very ironic that the teams and their physicians are trying [through testing] to help the professional athletes get off and stay off drugs and that the players' union is fighting the effort, treating it as if it were a bargaining chip."

Bergfeld, team physician for both the Cleveland Browns of the NFL and the Cleveland Cavaliers of the NBA as well as a consultant to the Cleveland Indians of MLB, agrees with Zairns, noting that athletes are better off than many employees. "The professional athlete does not realize how lucky he is to have an enlightened management outlook and an enlightened medical outlook that gives him a second chance on drugs." Leach, head physician for the 1984 U.S. Olympic team and physician to the Boston Celtics of the NBA, notes that the job of making sure athletes are "clean" is not always easy. "We have the machinery to do the drug testing, but it will be a big challenge to assure uniform accuracy of testing across the country."

Drug-Testing Procedures

Many of the amateur and professional teams that try to detect the use of banned substances use the same tests, some of which cost up to $200 each. Usually, each athlete is asked to give a sample of urine in the presence of a testing official. Urine is used because it is a bodily fluid that can be obtained with a minimum of discomfort to the athlete and because it contains significant amounts of many banned substances for days after they are ingested. A portion of each sample is passed through an instrument called a thin-layer chromatograph. Different substances flow down a glass plate at different rates, according to how they interact with its specially coated surface. In this way, trained technicians can isolate and identify many different substances in a particular sample.

If extreme precision is needed, testers may make use of a gas chromatograph. This device first vaporizes the urine,

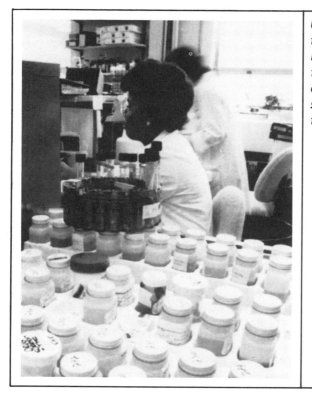

Urine samples being tested at a research laboratory. Urine is used to test for drugs because it contains many banned substances for weeks after they have been ingested.

then combines it with an inert (chemically inactive) gas, and finally passes the combination over a chemically treated column. This process separates the urine into its different components. After the gas has dissipated, technicians decipher the colorations left on the column to determine if any banned compounds are present.

A more accurate but somewhat more time consuming test than the gas chromatograph alone is the use of a mass spectrometer. In this instrument, some of the original urine sample is vaporized by a gas chromatograph and then ionized (converted to electrically active forms). By passing the gas through an electric current and a magnetic field, the different ions can be separated from each other by weight. Every substance has a unique "signature" in the mass spectrometer because it has a characteristic combination of molecules. By reading the electrical properties of the ions, it is possible to determine the chemical composition of a particular sample with great precision.

Using these three techniques, experts estimate that testers can determine when banned substances are present about 95% of the time. In order to cut down on the remaining 5% of uncertainty, testers may repeat the gas-chromatograph or the mass-spectrometer tests several times. In unusual circumstances, athletes may be asked to give a sample of blood, which is analyzed using the same techniques. This is considered an "invasive" technique (a tester must get a blood sample directly from an athlete's vein) and is usually used only if athletes are suspected of tampering with the urine sample or of substituting someone else's urine for their own.

A fourth technique for drug testing also shows great promise. The EMIT (enzyme multiplied immunoassay technique) test may eventually prove more accurate than either the gas chromatograph or the mass spectrometer. The sub-

Chuck Muncie leaves the Miami Dolphins training camp in 1984 after failing a drug test required for all team members. Two years earlier the NFL had adopted a procedure calling for mandatory drug tests as part of the normal preseason physical exam.

stance that is being tested for (i.e., THC or cocaine) is injected into an animal in order to provoke its immune system into producing antibodies. An antibody is a substance produced by animals (including humans) that attacks a specific substance invading the body. These antibodies are collected, purified, and placed into a substance that allows them to remain active outside the animal's body. This constitutes the testing substance, which is then combined with a sample of the urine from an athlete to be tested. If the urine contains a banned drug, an immediate and visible reaction occurs. Because the body responds with a unique antibody for each threatening substance, it is possible to test with great accuracy for the presence of a specific substance. EMIT is emerging, for example, as the most sensitive test for the use of marijuana.

Some drugs stay in the body longer than others. Recognizable by-products of the active ingredient in marijuana can remain in the urine for up to 10 days after smoking, for example, while long-term users of marijuana may show traces of THC and substances into which it is broken down up to 30 days after the last use. Cocaine, on the other hand, is usually completely eliminated from the body three days after being used.

National Football League

In 1982 the NFL Players' Association and team owners adopted a procedure calling for all players to undergo a mandatory drug test before the season starts, as part of the normal preseason physical. If an NFL player tests positive for a banned substance or if the team doctor has reasonable cause to believe any player is using drugs, tests may be ordered during the season. If a player is found to be using a banned substance, he is required to undergo drug counseling.

In July 1986 Pete Rozelle, commissioner of the NFL, announced a proposal for newer, more stringent drug testing. In place of the old plan, which he called "ineffective," Rozelle called for at least three urine tests per player per season — one at the beginning of the season and two others at unscheduled times. Rozelle also called for counseling and continued testing for 30 days following a positive test, a 30-day suspension at half pay after a second positive test, and dismissal without pay following a third positive test. Rozelle's plan specifically banned the use of cocaine, marijuana, opiates, and phencyclidine hydrochloride (PCP), and it offered warnings about steroids, amphetamines, and excessive use of alcohol.

Many of the NFL's coaches and players seemed to be in favor of Rozelle's proposal for stronger antidrug measures. In one poll of the Houston Oilers, for example, 57% of the players said they favored random drug testing, while 43% opposed it. Despite these statistics the NFL Players' Association opposed Rozelle's changes on the grounds that any league policy that affects the players must be part of an overall collective-bargaining agreement among the league, the owners, and the players. The Players' Association announced their own version of an antidrug plan, calling for the continuation of the same testing schedule as under the previous agreement but imposing harsher penalties for failing the drug tests. In October 1986 an arbitrator ruled in favor of the Players' Association on the drug-testing issue. The NFL, therefore, will remain under the rules of the former collective-bargaining agreement until it expires in 1987. Drug testing of NFL prospects, conducted prior to the annual collegiate draft, will be under league supervision.

Major League Baseball

Similar negotiating problems plague drug testing in baseball. In May 1984 the office of the commissioner put together a "memorandum of agreement" on drug testing of players that would cover narcotics, cocaine, marijuana, and at least 20 other drugs. The agreement calls for testing a player when a team has reason to believe that he is using one of the prohibited substances as well as mandatory penalties when players test positive. So far the agreement has not been ratified by the players.

On opening day of the 1986 baseball season, Commissioner Peter Ueberroth sent a letter to all major league players informing them of a proposed plan to test the urine of ball players four times each year for cocaine, marijuana, and the narcotics heroin and morphine. The plan was similar to one Ueberroth had imposed on minor league players and the umpires' union. As with the NFL, the Major League Baseball Players' Association vehemently opposed the plan, not because it was against drug testing but because Ueberroth failed to obtain the agreement through bargaining with the players' union. "He doesn't have the authority to impose [such a plan]," said Donald Fehr, executive director of the Players' Association.

Some teams, interested in ensuring the health of the players, negotiated the issue of drug testing directly with them. Since there was no general agreement with the union, teams began writing clauses into the contracts of some players authorizing mandatory drug testing. There was speculation around the league that this practice might become standard. By March 1986 some 40% of players had the clauses in their contracts. Later in the year, however, an independent arbitrator declared both Ueberroth's drug-testing plan and the separate contracts invalid because they had not been negotiated with the players' union. As of 1987 there is still no agreement, although the subject is likely to come up for review when the league and the players negotiate a new collective-bargaining agreement in 1988.

Commissioner Peter Ueberroth has been unable to institute an official drug-testing program for Major League Baseball. Nevertheless, according to Ueberroth, drug use among players is on the decline.

Since there is no agreement, teams and players thus far have handled the testing issue on a case-by-case basis. No one has been banned from playing major league baseball, although several players have been assessed penalties and publicly reprimanded for using drugs such as marijuana and cocaine. (See Chapter 2.)

Ironically, all of the bad publicity concerning the use of drugs by baseball players may have furthered reform efforts more than an agreement between the league and the players. Ueberroth is convinced that much progress has already been made toward stemming the tide of drugs in baseball. At a hearing before the House Select Committee on Narcotic Abuse and Control in May 1986 he said: "Baseball is defeating the problem. Frankly, the battle is over. There might be a flare-up or two from time to time, but the institution of baseball has returned dignity to itself. You're not going to hear about any baseball scandals from this day forward."

Other Professional Sports

There is no general agreement concerning drug testing between the league and the players in the National Hockey League (NHL), but there is widespread support for strong measures regarding drug abuse. Superstar Wayne Gretzky of the Edmonton Oilers, for example, who has already appeared in antidrug commercials on television, advocates drug testing. "I think it should be brought in, although I can't speak for every guy in the league," Gretzky has been quoted as saying.

In fact, in early 1986 allegations of drug use among Gretzky's Edmonton teammates surfaced. NHL President John Ziegler denied that there was a major problem with the Oilers or in the league in general. Commenting on the specific allegations against the Oilers, Ziegler noted, "We do not have and have not had any evidence of drug use by any of our players." Nevertheless, after the conclusion of the 1985–86 season, Ziegler proposed a new drug-testing program. The proposal has yet to be ratified by the players but includes provisions for education and counseling of offenders. "Since 1978, our policy has been that if you use drugs, and you get caught, you get suspended," Ziegler said after making the announcement.

In contrast to the wrangling that has characterized negotiations over specific aspects of drug-testing procedures in other professional sports organizations, the NBA, in 1983, established a stringent set of procedures to deal with drug abuse that is supported by team owners and players alike. Under these procedures, a player may twice voluntarily request assistance with a drug problem. (The NBA program concerns only heroin and cocaine.) The player's team will then pay for his counseling and medical assistance and require him to complete an extensive program of rehabilitation and follow-up care. A lifetime ban results in the following circumstances: if a player is involved a third time with heroin or cocaine, even if such use is voluntarily disclosed; if a player tests positive after undergoing drug testing authorized by the league's drug expert after this expert receives reliable information that the player is using drugs; if a player who has undergone drug treatment misses a game or a combination of two practices and/or two team flights within a week and tests positive after undergoing urinalysis; or if a player is convicted of a crime involving the use of heroin or cocaine. (As we mentioned earlier, several NBA players have already been banned from basketball under the provisions of this agreement on drug testing.)

Professional track athletes have come increasingly under the scrutiny of drug testing. In October 1986 officials of the prestigious New York Marathon announced that in accordance with guidelines set by The Athletics Congress (TAC), which is the governing body for track and field in this country, the top three male and female finishers, as well as two other finishers randomly selected from among the top 25, would be subjected to tests for drugs such as amphetamines and steroids. Fred Lebow, director of the race, announced the tests in response to past suspicions of drug use among top finishers. "I think we have a moral obligation in a mass participation sport where prize money is given to see that no one cheats," Lebow said in an interview with *The New York Times*. The second-place finisher in the 1986 race, Antoni Niemczak of Poland, was disqualified after a postrace urinalysis revealed that he had used a banned steroid substance.

Amateur Athletics

Some experts felt that amateur athletics in this country were dealt an embarrassing blow when some participants in the 1983 Pan American Games withdrew from competition

National Hockey League President John Ziegler has proposed a procedure for drug testing among hockey players, but the program has yet to be ratified.

rather than face drug testing. The current policy is that American athletes who want to compete internationally have to undergo tests for the use of illegal drugs that are just as rigorous as their training programs.

In April 1986 Robert Helmick, president of the U.S. Olympic Committee (USOC), announced that all 38 governing bodies of amateur sports in the United States had agreed to mandatory drug testing for all athletes. Helmick stressed that up to 3,000 amateur athletes were expected to be tested by the end of 1986, in addition to 3,500 who had been tested prior to 1986. Physician Robert Voy, the chief medical officer of the USOC, agrees that the new plan should help. "We're leading the way with a tough program," Voy said. Under the USOC's plan, athletes who fail a urinalysis test twice face penalties ranging from a six-month to life ban from U.S. Olympic events.

The new USOC guidelines call for testing of any athletes likely to qualify for international competition (including alternates), as well as one-fifth of the remaining participants in all events. The testing is to take place immediately following the competition, and a testing official is present during every phase of the testing. Two separate specimens are collected from each athlete. In the event of a positive test, the second specimen is analyzed as an automatic appeal on the athlete's behalf. Any athlete who does not cooperate or refuses to be tested is disqualified. The USOC testing program currently prohibits the use of more than 3,300 different prescription, over-the-counter, and illegal substances. Representatives of all major drug classes, including narcotics and painkillers, steroids, alcohol, beta-blockers, anesthetics, corticosteroids, diuretics, and caffeine, are on the list.

The tighter testing procedures are already in place. In October 1986 TAC suspended 25-year-old discus thrower Rick Meyer, who had placed first during the U.S. Olympic Festival in Houston in August. TAC did not announce the drug test Meyer had failed, but he became the fourth competitor in 1986 to be banned by TAC from further sanctioned competition.

College athletes are also being more closely tested. In the fall of 1986 the NCAA began a random drug-testing program in all 73 championships overseen by the association. Any athlete who tests positive for one of 200 banned drugs will become ineligible for further competition for three months. In addition, an athlete who tests positive will cause his or her entire team to be disqualified from the championship. "We want to rid our sports and our student-athletes of drugs," Jack Davis, the NCAA president, said. "We think the institution and the team should bear some responsibility if one of its players is found to be using drugs."

John B. Slaughter, chancellor of the University of Maryland, announced in June 1986 that he had begun spearheading a drive among Division I schools to increase testing. "We will contact [representatives from other schools] and call their attention to the need for taking a much more aggressive stance," he said. Slaughter admitted that the death of Len Bias had in part motivated his initiative, but he insisted that the need for stronger testing went beyond that individual tragedy. "The issue is that we are faced with a very serious situation. We are at war with drugs."

The efforts of Slaughter and others are beginning to pay off. In 1986 David Cook and Raymond Tricker, both of whom are members of the physical education department at the University of Kansas, questioned 44 head athletic trainers at Division I schools of the NCAA about their school's policy on drug testing. Every school they contacted tests athletes for using marijuana and cocaine, and almost all test for barbiturates and anabolic steroids. Two-thirds now also test for steroid abuse, and slightly less than half test for excessive alcohol consumption and abuse of muscle relaxants.

Significantly, two out of every five schools surveyed said that athletes who tested positive three times would be kicked off their team and risk losing their scholarship. Cook and Tricker also noted that more than half of the trainers agreed that "the athletes have a positive attitude toward the school's drug testing program." Seventy percent of the coaches felt that the drug-testing program "has deterred athletes from experimenting with drugs in general," and 83% agreed that the program had a positive effect in reducing the use of drugs for which the tests were designed.

Drug Testing Abroad

Some athletes in other countries are now also being tested. For years observers believed that marijuana use was rampant among professional soccer players in Kenya. According to some accounts, 90% of the players used the drug and were being encouraged by their coaches to do so. In February 1986 Job Omino, chairman of the Kenyan Football Federation, announced a random blood- and urine-testing program for the 20 teams in the league. "We have no alternative but to clamp down on this pathetic situation," Omino said. "It is a matter of national concern."

In Great Britain amateur golfers are now being routinely tested for drug use. Keith Wright, an official of the English Golf Union, announced the tests in March 1986, after they had been ordered by Britain's Sports Council, even though in his words, "As far as we know, there is no benefit that can be derived from drugs on the golf course," Wright said.

Canadian athletes are also running into stiffer drug testing. In July 1986 three of the country's top track-and-field competitors tested positive for drug use and were banned from competition by the Canadian Track and Field Association. One, Rob Gray, was the country's national discus cham-

Scottish soccer player Willie Johnston Smith tested positive for drugs during the 1978 World Cup competition.

pion before being disqualified. Although Gray and his teammates disputed the results of the drug test, the suspensions have been upheld by further tests.

Drug Testing and Civil Rights

Regardless of whether or not drug testing is effective in minimizing drug abuse inside the sports community and among other segments of the population, serious questions have been raised, from the civil libertarian standpoint, about its legality.

Irving Kaufman, a judge on the U.S. Court of Appeals for the Second Circuit, addressed the question in an article in *The New York Times Magazine* in October 1986. According to Kaufman, "drug testing is shaping up as the premier issue in labor relations for the next decade."

The central issue on which drug testing may be challenged is an individual's right to privacy, guaranteed to all Americans by the Fourth Amendment of the Constitution: "The right of the people to be secure in their persons, houses, papers and effects, against unreasonable searches and sei-

Lebanese weightlifter Mahmoud Tarha was banned from the 1984 Olympic Games after testing positive for drugs. Drug testing is required of all Olympic athletes; refusal to cooperate means disqualification.

zures, shall not be violated. . . ." Of course, there are instances when people must forfeit the right to absolute privacy, such as when they agree to be searched before boarding an airplane. According to Kaufman, the legality of drug testing "may hinge in part on the purpose to which the program is put": drug testing used to identify and rehabilitate drug users may be allowed, while drug testing primarily to investigate possible illegal activity probably will not. There have already been cases in which courts of law have decided that asking government employees to submit to urinalysis is an invasion of privacy if there is no reason to suspect them of using drugs in the first place.

Although professional athletic leagues and amateur athletic associations are private corporations and not subject to the provisions of the Fourth Amendment in the same way as is the federal government, these decisions and policies may have some application to them. In the future teams and associations that seek to test athletes may need to show some reason to suspect an athlete of drug use before they test them. In addition officials may be required to show genuine interest in the health and well-being of those they test besides simply stating the desire to keep athletics "drug-free."

Judge Kaufman points out that so far "the debate on drug screening has been rich in emotion and hyperbole." Let us hope that, at least as far as athletes and athletics are concerned, the issue can be resolved in a way that ensures the health and safety of athletes without unduly infringing on their personal rights.

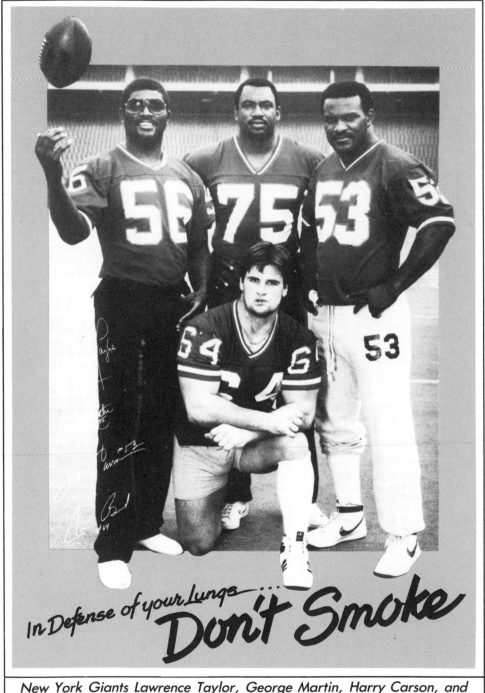

In Defense of your Lungs... *Don't Smoke*

New York Giants Lawrence Taylor, George Martin, Harry Carson, and Jim Burt posed for this antismoking poster in 1985. More and more athletes are lending their prestige to the war against drug abuse.

CHAPTER 6

TREATING DRUG
ABUSERS

Working under the assumption that the best treatment for drug abuse is prevention, all of the major sports leagues, including the NBA, NFL, NHL, and MLB, have educational programs that strive to teach players about meeting the challenge of drug use. This can sometimes be as critical for professionals as it is for younger athletes. Even highly paid pros come in contact with "friends," "fans," or "well-wishers" who encourage them to use drugs. Psychologist Arthur MacNeill Horton, however, argues that it would be far better to try to encourage athletes to maintain healthy social-support systems. "An awful lot of research on preventive strategies shows that education programs just cause the subjects to use more drugs," he says. "It is hard to change people's beliefs."

Despite the best wishes of parents and coaches, and often despite the wishes of the competitors themselves, there have always been a number of athletes who run into problems with drugs. A variety of methods have been developed to deal with those who are unable to handle their own drug difficulties.

When Micheal Ray Richardson was banned from the NBA, he reported on more than one occasion to a center specializing in treating those addicted to drugs. Each time he failed to cure his cocaine habit. According to Horton, a spe-

Micheal Ray Richardson repeatedly failed to overcome his cocaine addiction and was consequently banned from NBA competition.

cialist in alcohol and polyaddictions (those addicted to several substances simultaneously), this is not unusual. "I usually expect only about five percent of those who begin treatment programs for addictions to be completely successful over the long run," he says. "This doesn't reflect on Richardson's dedication nor on the desires of his team and the NBA to cure him. It simply represents the fact that no program we have right now to treat addictions is very good."

Horton cautions those who are tempted to use drugs in the mistaken belief that they can easily give them up later if problems develop. "I would have to say that the success rate [for treating addiction] is very dismal, if you look at it from a long-term point of view. We have an abysmal lack of knowledge of what might be effective for these individuals."

Nevertheless, Horton and others make use of a broad range of techniques to try to rid users of their addictions. This process is usually divided into two stages. The first is detoxification or "detox." During a period of a few days (that can sometimes stretch to a few weeks), drug users stop taking the drug or drugs to which they have become accustomed and are helped through any overdose complications or withdrawal symptoms they may suffer.

The second phase of treatment usually involves psychotherapy. Some therapy takes place in a psychiatrist's or psychologist's office. The therapists help users understand the nature of their problem and how it has come to run their lives. "I try to develop a relationship with [an abuser]," Horton says. "I work with the emotions and confront the facts of the abuse to help an addict realize that things have gotten out of control." If the abuser is younger than 18, the therapy usually includes the parents. "Often, part of the reason for the drug abuse is a poor family environment," Horton says.

Planning a Recovery Strategy

Therapists are responsible for helping addicts plan their own recovery strategy, to set up specific goals and expectations for themselves. According to psychologist Gilbert Botvin of Cornell University, this sometimes means dealing with other problems — such as abnormal sexuality, poor care for oneself, lack of assertiveness, uncontrolled impulses, and impotence — that sometimes accompany drug addiction. This approach is often, but not always, effective. "It is important to remember that treating [other problems] may not eliminate drug abuse and resolution of these problems is not essential for a drug-free state," Botvin says.

Inevitably, the therapist and client have to deal with relapse — the times that drug users backslide and begin their old habits. "Star athletes may have special problems in this area," says Horton, coordinator of the alcoholism program at the Veterans Administration Medical Center in Baltimore, Maryland. "Because they feel superior to everyone else and because they know that they may earn in one year several times what you and I earn in a lifetime, they may feel especially invulnerable to drugs."

Hazelden-Cork Center

The setting for rehabilitation treatment is usually a medical institution of some kind. One of the best drug-abuse treatment facilities in the country for athletes is the Hazelden-Cork Center in Minnesota. Hazelden-Cork sponsors a series of workshops, clinics, and education programs for coaches, trainers, and both amateur and professional athletes. The Hazelden Foundation was founded in 1949 and is internationally known for its efforts in chemical dependence, training, education, therapy, and research. Operation Cork was founded in 1976 by Joan Kroc, widow of Ray Kroc (the founder of the McDonald's Corporation and former owner of the San Diego Padres baseball team).

In 1984 Cork and Hazelden jointly established a $6.9 million state-of-the-art facility in Center City, Minnesota, for the treatment and education of drug abusers. There athletes can learn to cope with life without relying on alcohol and drugs. "Through our experience of working with those involved in athletics at the professional, college, and high school level, we have gained a good understanding of the opportunity athletic programs provide to work with young people on chemical use issues," says Mark Lucas, outreach coordinator of the Hazelden-Cork Sports Education Program.

The Hazelden-Cork Center, a rehabilitation center in Minnesota, applies methods of counseling, education, and training to help both amateur and professional athletes overcome their drug dependencies.

Pittsburgh Pirates pitcher Rod Scurry met with reporters in 1984 after undergoing successful rehabilitation for cocaine addiction. Scurry subsequently returned to the Pirates.

Employee Assistance Programs

In 1981 Operation Cork created a drug-treatment program for the San Diego Padres. Since then Cork has established similar programs for a variety of companies, institutions, and organizations. An integral part of the program Cork established for the Padres is called the "Employee Assistance Program," or EAP. Any player with a drug problem may, without penalty or cost, refer himself to professional treatment and counseling, put in place by the team.

In professional sports and elsewhere, EAPs are catching on as a remarkably effective way of treating alcoholism and drug abuse. In August 1986 the National Institute on Alcohol Abuse and Alcoholism reported on 480 companies in six states that have EAPs covering more than 3 million employees. According to the study, a high rate of employees with alcohol problems returned to their jobs, and EAPs may be "prototypes of occupational medical departments of the fu-

The body of a trained athlete is a machine that must function under punishing stress. Ultimately, the energy and endurance that sustain this performance can come only from the body itself — not from drugs.

ture." Within 12 months after going into treatment programs, "an average of 70% of the cases, or 8,553 employees, with drinking problems were back on the job and performing adequately," the study said.

Another source of treatment for those with substance-abuse problems are self-help groups such as Alcoholics Anonymous and Narcotics Anonymous. These organizations have helped many alcoholics and drug addicts on the long road to recovery.

In short, there are a variety of programs now in place to help athletes and others recover from their drug-abuse problems. However, addiction is cruelly tenacious, and no form of treatment has anything but a limited rate of success. "People who think that we have come a long way in terms of drug treatment programs are wrong," Horton says. "They are deluding themselves."

Conclusion

By one estimate, drug abuse costs the businesses of the United States at least $85 million every year in lost productivity. It also degrades the quality of millions and millions of lives. Yet as often as we hear such facts and statistics, they do not bring the reality of this national problem home with the same force as an isolated, individual tragedy. In an eerie prediction, physician Arnold Beckett of Chelsea College at the University of London wrote in 1983 that "it may take a death in sport through drug misuse to galvanize people" into doing something about drug abuse among athletes. More than the most chilling barrage of statistics, spectacular deaths may finally encourage great change. It is a sad legacy that Len Bias has left, but it is up to us to make his death the occasion for meaningful change.

APPENDIX

State Agencies
for the Prevention and Treatment
of Drug Abuse

ALABAMA
Department of Mental Health
Division of Mental Illness and
    Substance Abuse Community
    Programs
200 Interstate Park Drive
P.O. Box 3710
Montgomery, AL 36193
(205) 271-9253

ALASKA
Department of Health and Social
    Services
Office of Alcoholism and Drug
    Abuse
Pouch H-05-F
Juneau, AK 99811
(907) 586-6201

ARIZONA
Department of Health Services
Division of Behavioral Health
    Services
Bureau of Community Services
Alcohol Abuse and Alcoholism
    Section
2500 East Van Buren
Phoenix, AZ 85008
(602) 255-1238

Department of Health Services
Division of Behavioral Health
    Services
Bureau of Community Services
Drug Abuse Section
2500 East Van Buren
Phoenix, AZ 85008
(602) 255-1240

ARKANSAS
Department of Human Services
Office of Alcohol and Drug Abuse
    Prevention
1515 West 7th Avenue
Suite 310
Little Rock, AR 72202
(501) 371-2603

CALIFORNIA
Department of Alcohol and Drug
    Abuse
111 Capitol Mall
Sacramento, CA 95814
(916) 445-1940

COLORADO
Department of Health
Alcohol and Drug Abuse Division
4210 East 11th Avenue
Denver, CO 80220
(303) 320-6137

CONNECTICUT
Alcohol and Drug Abuse
    Commission
999 Asylum Avenue
3rd Floor
Hartford, CT 06105
(203) 566-4145

DELAWARE
Division of Mental Health
Bureau of Alcoholism and Drug
    Abuse
1901 North Dupont Highway
Newcastle, DE 19720
(302) 421-6101

DISTRICT OF COLUMBIA
Department of Human Services
Office of Health Planning and
  Development
601 Indiana Avenue, NW
Suite 500
Washington, D.C. 20004
(202) 724-5641

FLORIDA
Department of Health and
  Rehabilitative Services
Alcoholic Rehabilitation Program
1317 Winewood Boulevard
Room 187A
Tallahassee, FL 32301
(904) 488-0396

Department of Health and
  Rehabilitative Services
Drug Abuse Program
1317 Winewood Boulevard
Building 6, Room 155
Tallahassee, FL 32301
(904) 488-0900

GEORGIA
Department of Human Resources
Division of Mental Health and
  Mental Retardation
Alcohol and Drug Section
618 Ponce De Leon Avenue, NE
Atlanta, GA 30365-2101
(404) 894-4785

HAWAII
Department of Health
Mental Health Division
Alcohol and Drug Abuse Branch
1250 Punch Bowl Street
P.O. Box 3378
Honolulu, HI 96801
(808) 548-4280

IDAHO
Department of Health and Welfare
Bureau of Preventive Medicine
Substance Abuse Section
450 West State
Boise, ID 83720
(208) 334-4368

ILLINOIS
Department of Mental Health and
  Developmental Disabilities
Division of Alcoholism
160 North La Salle Street
Room 1500
Chicago, IL 60601
(312) 793-2907

Illinois Dangerous Drugs
  Commission
300 North State Street
Suite 1500
Chicago, IL 60610
(312) 822-9860

INDIANA
Department of Mental Health
Division of Addiction Services
429 North Pennsylvania Street
Indianapolis, IN 46204
(317) 232-7816

IOWA
Department of Substance Abuse
505 5th Avenue
Insurance Exchange Building
Suite 202
Des Moines, IA 50319
(515) 281-3641

KANSAS
Department of Social Rehabilitation
Alcohol and Drug Abuse Services
2700 West 6th Street
Biddle Building
Topeka, KS 66606
(913) 296-3925

KENTUCKY
Cabinet for Human Resources
Department of Health Services
Substance Abuse Branch
275 East Main Street
Frankfort, KY 40601
(502) 564-2880

LOUISIANA
Department of Health and Human
  Resources
Office of Mental Health and
  Substance Abuse
655 North 5th Street
P.O. Box 4049
Baton Rouge, LA 70821
(504) 342-2565

MAINE
Department of Human Services
Office of Alcoholism and Drug
  Abuse Prevention
Bureau of Rehabilitation
32 Winthrop Street
Augusta, ME 04330
(207) 289-2781

MARYLAND
Alcoholism Control Administration
201 West Preston Street
Fourth Floor
Baltimore, MD 21201
(301) 383-2977

State Health Department
Drug Abuse Administration
201 West Preston Street
Baltimore, MD 21201
(301) 383-3312

MASSACHUSETTS
Department of Public Health
Division of Alcoholism
755 Boylston Street
Sixth Floor
Boston, MA 02116
(617) 727-1960

Department of Public Health
Division of Drug Rehabilitation
600 Washington Street
Boston, MA 02114
(617) 727-8617

MICHIGAN
Department of Public Health
Office of Substance Abuse Services
3500 North Logan Street
P.O. Box 30035
Lansing, MI 48909
(517) 373-8603

MINNESOTA
Department of Public Welfare
Chemical Dependency Program
  Division
Centennial Building
658 Cedar Street
4th Floor
Saint Paul, MN 55155
(612) 296-4614

MISSISSIPPI
Department of Mental Health
Division of Alcohol and Drug Abuse
1102 Robert E. Lee Building
Jackson, MS 39201
(601) 359-1297

MISSOURI
Department of Mental Health
Division of Alcoholism and Drug
  Abuse
2002 Missouri Boulevard
P.O. Box 687
Jefferson City, MO 65102
(314) 751-4942

MONTANA
Department of Institutions
Alcohol and Drug Abuse Division
1539 11th Avenue
Helena, MT 59620
(406) 449-2827

NEBRASKA
Department of Public Institutions
Division of Alcoholism and Drug
Abuse
801 West Van Dorn Street
P.O. Box 94728
Lincoln, NB 68509
(402) 471-2851, Ext. 415

NEVADA
Department of Human Resources
Bureau of Alcohol and Drug Abuse
505 East King Street
Carson City, NV 89710
(702) 885-4790

NEW HAMPSHIRE
Department of Health and Welfare
Office of Alcohol and Drug Abuse
    Prevention
Hazen Drive
Health and Welfare Building
Concord, NH 03301
(603) 271-4627

NEW JERSEY
Department of Health
Division of Alcoholism
129 East Hanover Street CN 362
Trenton, NJ 08625
(609) 292-8949

Department of Health
Division of Narcotic and Drug
    Abuse Control
129 East Hanover Street CN 362
Trenton, NJ 08625
(609) 292-8949

NEW MEXICO
Health and Environment Department
Behavioral Services Division
Substance Abuse Bureau
725 Saint Michaels Drive
P.O. Box 968
Santa Fe, NM 87503
(505) 984-0020, Ext. 304

NEW YORK
Division of Alcoholism and Alcohol
    Abuse
194 Washington Avenue
Albany, NY 12210
(518) 474-5417

Division of Substance Abuse
    Services
Executive Park South
Box 8200
Albany, NY 12203
(518) 457-7629

NORTH CAROLINA
Department of Human Resources
Division of Mental Health, Mental
    Retardation and Substance Abuse
    Services
Alcohol and Drug Abuse Services
325 North Salisbury Street
Albemarle Building
Raleigh, NC 27611
(919) 733-4670

NORTH DAKOTA
Department of Human Services
Division of Alcoholism and Drug
    Abuse
State Capitol Building
Bismarck, ND 58505
(701) 224-2767

OHIO
Department of Health
Division of Alcoholism
246 North High Street
P.O. Box 118
Columbus, OH 43216
(614) 466-3543

Department of Mental Health
Bureau of Drug Abuse
65 South Front Street
Columbus, OH 43215
(614) 466-9023

OKLAHOMA
Department of Mental Health
Alcohol and Drug Programs
4545 North Lincoln Boulevard
Suite 100 East Terrace
P.O. Box 53277
Oklahoma City, OK 73152
(405) 521-0044

OREGON
Department of Human Resources
Mental Health Division
Office of Programs for Alcohol and
   Drug Problems
2575 Bittern Street, NE
Salem, OR 97310
(503) 378-2163

PENNSYLVANIA
Department of Health
Office of Drug and Alcohol
   Programs
Commonwealth and Forster Avenues
Health and Welfare Building
P.O. Box 90
Harrisburg, PA 17108
(717) 787-9857

RHODE ISLAND
Department of Mental Health,
   Mental Retardation and Hospitals
Division of Substance Abuse
Substance Abuse Administration
   Building
Cranston, RI 02920
(401) 464-2091

SOUTH CAROLINA
Commission on Alcohol and Drug
   Abuse
3700 Forest Drive
Columbia, SC 29204
(803) 758-2521

SOUTH DAKOTA
Department of Health
Division of Alcohol and Drug Abuse
523 East Capitol, Joe Foss Building
Pierre, SD 57501
(605) 773-4806

TENNESSEE
Department of Mental Health and
   Mental Retardation
Alcohol and Drug Abuse Services
505 Deaderick Street
James K. Polk Building,
   Fourth Floor
Nashville, TN 37219
(615) 741-1921

TEXAS
Commission on Alcoholism
809 Sam Houston State Office
   Building
Austin, TX 78701
(512) 475-2577
Department of Community Affairs
Drug Abuse Prevention Division
2015 South Interstate Highway 35
P.O. Box 13166
Austin, TX 78711
(512) 443-4100

UTAH
Department of Social Services
Division of Alcoholism and Drugs
150 West North Temple
Suite 350
P.O. Box 2500
Salt Lake City, UT 84110
(801) 533-6532

VERMONT
Agency of Human Services
Department of Social and
   Rehabilitation Services
Alcohol and Drug Abuse Division
103 South Main Street
Waterbury, VT 05676
(802) 241-2170

VIRGINIA
Department of Mental Health and
Mental Retardation
Division of Substance Abuse
109 Governor Street
P.O. Box 1797
Richmond, VA 23214
(804) 786-5313

WASHINGTON
Department of Social and Health
Service
Bureau of Alcohol and Substance
Abuse
Office Building—44 W
Olympia, WA 98504
(206) 753-5866

WEST VIRGINIA
Department of Health
Office of Behavioral Health Services
Division on Alcoholism and Drug
Abuse
1800 Washington Street East
Building 3 Room 451
Charleston, WV 25305
(304) 348-2276

WISCONSIN
Department of Health and Social
Services
Division of Community Services
Bureau of Community Programs
Alcohol and Other Drug Abuse
Program Office
1 West Wilson Street
P.O. Box 7851
Madison, WI 53707
(608) 266-2717

WYOMING
Alcohol and Drug Abuse Programs
Hathaway Building
Cheyenne, WY 82002
(307) 777-7115, Ext. 7118

GUAM
Mental Health & Substance Abuse
Agency
P.O. Box 20999
Guam 96921

PUERTO RICO
Department of Addiction Control
Services
Alcohol Abuse Programs
P.O. Box B-Y Rio Piedras Station
Rio Piedras, PR 00928
(809) 763-5014

Department of Addiction Control
Services
Drug Abuse Programs
P.O. Box B-Y Rio Piedras Station
Rio Piedras, PR 00928
(809) 764-8140

VIRGIN ISLANDS
Division of Mental Health,
Alcoholism & Drug Dependency
Services
P.O. Box 7329
Saint Thomas, Virgin Islands 00801
(809) 774-7265

AMERICAN SAMOA
LBJ Tropical Medical Center
Department of Mental Health Clinic
Pago Pago, American Samoa 96799

TRUST TERRITORIES
Director of Health Services
Office of the High Commissioner
Saipan, Trust Territories 96950

Further Reading

Cohen, Sidney, and O'Brien, Robert. *The Encyclopedia of Drug Abuse*. New York: Facts on File, 1984.

Donohoe, Tom, and Johnson, Neil. *Foul Play: Drug Abuse in Sports*. London: Basil Blackwell, 1986.

Goldman, Bob, et al. *Death in the Locker Room: Steroids and Sports*. New York: Century Publishing Co., Inc., 1984.

Haycock, Christine E. *Sports Medicine for the Female Athlete*. New York: Perigee Books, 1980.

Podell, Janet, ed. *Sports in America*. New York: H. W. Wilson Company, 1986.

Torrey, Lee. *Stretching the Limits: Breakthroughs in Sports Science That Create Super Athletes*. New York: Dodd, Mead & Company, 1986.

Glossary

addiction a condition caused by repeated drug use, characterized by a compulsive urge to continue using the drug, a tendency to increase the dosage, and physiological and/or psychological dependence

adrenal gland a ductless gland situated on top of the kidney that secretes adrenaline

adrenaline a hormone released in times of stress; also referred to as epinephrine

analgesia reduction of the ability to feel pain while still conscious

anesthesia the reduction or loss of sensation induced by certain drugs

antibody a protein produced by the circulatory system that attacks and eliminates foreign substances in the blood

arousal a complex physical state, usually the response to great exertion or fear, in which blood pressure and heart rate are increased

autonomic nervous system the part of the nervous system that is concerned with control of involuntary bodily functions

cardiovascular system the body system made up of the heart and the vessels carrying blood to and from it. There are three types of vessels: the arteries (which carry oxygen and nutrient-enriched blood from the heart to all parts of the body), the veins (which carry depleted blood back to the heart), and the capillaries (small vessels that connect veins and arteries)

chromatography the process of determining the composition of a particular mixed substance by analyzing differences in the components when they are separated. There are two principal means of chromatography: thin-layer chromatography and gas chromatography

cortex the outer layer of an organ (as opposed to the inner medulla), as in the adrenal gland, kidney, ovary, lymph, thymus, and cerebrum and cerebellum of the brain

dopamine a neurotransmitter synthesized by the adrenal gland that affects the autonomic nervous system

endocrine gland a ductless gland that produces a secretion discharged directly into the blood or lymph and then circulated to all parts of the body. The adrenals and testes are examples of endocrine glands

endorphins substances produced by the body enabling it to handle pain

ergogenic the term used to describe something that increases the potential for work output

euphoria a feeling of extreme well-being and overall elation

half life the time a body tissue or organ needs to metabolize half of a particular ingested substance

immune response a series of bodily responses to invasion by foreign bodies. The immune response normally involves the mobilization of the endocrine and circulatory systems and the production of antibodies

inoculation a term used in drug prevention to mean artificial exposure to a difficult situation in which a young person may be offered drugs. It is hoped that by exposing young people to such situations and teaching them how to say no, future drug use can be avoided

ligament a band of tough, flexible tissue that connects two bones together or holds an organ in place

lipid one of a large variety of fat or fatlike compounds that are insoluble in water. Some examples are waxes and cholesterol

motor skills a variety of human abilities under conscious control that involve physical action such as walking, picking up boxes, and stacking objects

muscle tissue made up of contractible cells or fibers that enable an organ or part of the body to greatly expand or contract

nervous system all of the nerve cells in the body, interlaced with one another, as well as the brain and spinal cord. This system regulates and coordinates body activities and responds to stimuli affecting sensory organs

neurotransmitter the chemical substances that are released by one neuron to transmit impulses to the receptors of other neurons. Many psychoactive drugs work on the body by mimicking, preventing, prolonging, or enhancing the actions of certain neurotransmitters

overdose the amount of a drug (which varies from person to person and from drug to drug) that when taken produces an acute or life-threatening condition

oxygen debt the amount of oxygen required after muscular activity to remove lactic acid and other metabolic products that have built up in the body as a result of increased exertion

parasympathetic nervous system part of the autonomic nervous system that performs specific functions which allow for certain involuntary responses, such as constriction of the pupils

perception the process by which we are consciously aware of the world around us through sensory impressions such as sight, hearing, taste, smell, and touch

physical dependence adaption of the body to the presence of a drug such that its absence produces withdrawal symptoms

physiological a term used to describe the effect that a drug or other stimulus has in purely physical terms on body functions

pituitary gland a small endocrine gland attached to the base of the brain that secretes hormones that regulate many body processes, including growth and reproduction

placebo a harmless substance in the form of a pill that may often be given to patients in a control group during drug experiments

psychological dependence a condition in which a drug user craves a drug to maintain a sense of well-being and feels discomfort when deprived of it

psychomotor skills a term used to describe human activity that is tied to mental processes. Some examples of these skills are reading, writing, and speaking

random testing the testing of a certain percentage of athletes participating at a sporting event for evidence of drug use that may affect their performance

reflex an immediate and involuntary response to a stimulus, such as pulling one's hand away from a fire

sympathetic nervous system a part of the autonomic nervous system that slows the digestive system and speeds up most other body functions, including heart rate and liver function

sympathomimetic drugs that imitate the neurotransmitters norepinephrine and epinephrine and cause activation of the sympathetic nervous system

tendon a mass of fibrous connective tissue attaching muscles to bones

therapeutic having medicinal or healing properties

tolerance a decrease of susceptibility to the effects of a drug due to its continued administration, resulting in the user's need to increase the drug's dosage in order to achieve desired effects

user a person who eats, drinks, smokes, or injects a drug

withdrawal the physiological and psychological effects of discontinued use of a drug

Picture Credits

Index

Jeff Meer is currently an assistant editor at *Psychology Today* and has worked at several other leading magazines. He holds a B.A. from Dartmouth College in French language and literature.

Solomon H. Snyder, M.D. is Distinguished Service Professor of Neuroscience, Pharmacology and Psychiatry at The Johns Hopkins University School of Medicine. He has served as president of the Society for Neuroscience and in 1978 received the Albert Lasker Award in Medical Research. He has authored *Uses of Marijuana, Madness and the Brain, The Troubled Mind, Biological Aspects of Mental Disorder,* and edited *Perspective in Neuropharmacology: A Tribute to Julius Axelrod.* Professor Snyder was a research associate with Dr. Axelrod at the National Institutes of Health.

Barry L. Jacobs, Ph.D., is currently a professor in the program of neuroscience at Princeton University. Professor Jacobs is author of *Serotonin Neurotransmission and Behavior* and *Hallucinogens: Neurochemical, Behavioral and Clinical Perspectives.* He has written many journal articles in the field of neuroscience and contributed numerous chapters to books on behavior and brain science. He has been a member of several panels of the National Institute of Mental Health.

Joann Ellison Rodgers, M.S. (Columbia), became Deputy Director of Public Affairs and Director of Media Relations for the Johns Hopkins Medical Institutions in Baltimore, Maryland, in 1984 after 18 years as an award-winning science journalist and widely read columnist for the Hearst newspapers.